Robyn Dylan

on Aug 17

@Karen Connell I think it is

real women with real experienc⌐ ⌐⌐⌐⌐ ⌐⌐⌐⌐ stories, the better.

Myra Graber

on Aug 17

@Karen Connell I think you are describing is divine timing. We all have hopes and dreams, but our desires are not fulfilled when we want them to; they are fulfilled when the time is right. Your story has something to teach. There is someone out there who needs your strength and the wisdom you gained from your experience.

Amanda Pile

on Aug 17

@Karen Connell you are writing about a subject where people really need support and proof that you can come through it and thrive - possibly even stronger than before. So many people just can't see the light at the end of the tunnel. Your book is needed!

Excellent introduction here, and amazing writing.
Overview: a polished, personal account of one woman's journey from a victim of trauma to an advocate for other victims of trauma.
Aim: To tell her story and incorporate resources and life lessons that will help battered women/victims of trauma
Excellent introduction here, and amazing writing.
Lauren Bittrock, Editor

us that nothing can silence truth."

Nancy Jo Perdue -
Comedy writer, journalist and renegade

Susan Ball, REAL Recovery After Abuse
susan@susanball.ca
www.recoveryafterabuse.ca

NNEDV: National Network To End Domestic Violence,
Washington, DC (202) 543-5566
Laura Zillman (202) 543-5566 x 211
Womenslaw.org
Techsafety.org

GAFTR Global Association for Trauma Recovery
(678) 568-9191
Tracey Osborne CEO/Founder tracey@gaftr.org
http://gaftr.org

NCADV National Coalition Against Domestic Violence
(303) 839-18/52
Denver, CO

VAWnet The Online Resource Center on Violence against Women (800) 537-2238

There is a growing awareness that men, in partnership with women, can play a significant role in ending violence against women. This has led to an increase in programs and activities that focus on men's roles in preventing violence against women. Men's anti-violence programs are informed by the understanding that violence against women hurts women and that men can have an important influence on reducing violence by changing their own attitudes and behavior and by intervening to prevent other men's violence.

among those women telling brief stories of our experiences living with domestic violence. Our stories are different: yet our stories are the same. Seldom told from the beginning, always told from the point of when the violence began and when it ended; if it ended.

Karen's book takes us on a journey through her life, seemingly almost perfect, and draws as slowly as she was drawn into the cycle of domestic violence. Her child was drawn into the inter-generational cycle of violence.

I am proud to say that we have remained close friends through the years. I know Karen to be a strong, resourceful woman. I applaud her perseverance and dedication to writing what is clearly a message to young women. The more we know the stronger we become. We all deserve to life a life free from violence or the threat of violence. Especially in our own home.

With grace and courage Karen allows us to share her story.

Peggie Reyna
Project Director, Deaf Services
Peace Over Violence

Beyond Surviving

Take Back Your Life
Using the Power of Choice

Karen Connell

Halo
PUBLISHING
INTERNATIONAL

ISBN: 978-1-63765-290-9
LCCN: 2022914431

Halo Publishing International, LLC
www.halopublishing.com

Printed and bound in the United States of America

As a survivor of extreme abuse, I was one of the first victims to publicly speak out against domestic violence.

As the Community Educator for Sojourn, I gave numerous television and radio interviews including both national and local programs and was a guest speaker in numerous college Women's Studies and Psychology classes.

I was honored by the City and County of Los Angeles, the governor of California and various domestic violence programs.

Along with other women working in this area, I lobbied for the first domestic violence bill, which became law, in California, in 1984.

Serving on the California Attorney General's Task Force comprised of Police, Sheriffs, Attorneys, Judges and Domestic Violence workers, we wrote the curriculum to train law enforcement how to properly respond to domestic violence calls.

I trained LAPD and other Los Angeles County law enforcement agencies.

While serving on the LA Domestic Violence Council I was recruited by the LA City Attorney's Office to create a Victim's Advocate program and oversee its implementation on a DOJ grant.

Contents

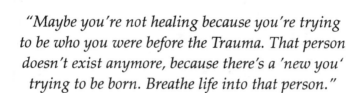

"Maybe you're not healing because you're trying to be who you were before the Trauma. That person doesn't exist anymore, because there's a 'new you' trying to be born. Breathe life into that person."

-Boli_ McCoy

Introduction

You Always Have a Choice

On May 2,1982, my life was changed abruptly and irrevocably. It set me on a path that would lead me to touch as many lives as possible and alert women everywhere to pay attention to what is going on around them and around their children. Children learn what a healthy relationship is largely based on their experiences at home. If they have good role models, they have a much better chance at having a healthy relationship, but that is not always the case. If they have someone in their life who models the ideas that violence is an acceptable way to control someone else, they will either grow up to replicate this behavior or shy away

consequently, want nothing to do with them.

As a formerly battered woman, I am finally chronicling how I went from being a victim in my own home to being on the forefront of the 1980's Domestic Violence Movement. Using my voice, which I feel is oftentimes barely above a whisper due to the violence I survived, I spoke out publicly about this insidious crime. Make no mistake; there is nothing quiet or orderly about intergenerational violence. It's the number-one crime of violence in the world and includes child abuse, spousal abuse, same-sex partner abuse, and elder abuse.

Calling it "domestic" is a way to soften the sound of the abuse, but I can promise you that there is nothing tame going on behind these closed doors. Just like the Black Lives Matter movement, this crime will have to move to the forefront of this country's consciousness if it's going to stop. Until the abusers, predominantly men, are educated to take responsibility for their violent behavior and stop blaming someone else, we cannot move forward.

As a rule, domestic violence has no boundaries. It crosses all lines, ages, races, classes, professions, sexual preferences, and religions. It affects one out of three women in this country, quite possibly the world. And that statistic is based only on reported cases.

As I set out to write this book (a book I have been encouraged to write for almost forty years), I can't believe, after all this time, that this crime has not only continued, but it's worse now than it was in the 1980s. On the nightly and possibly even himself are broadcast on your television. Sometimes, the man will kidnap his child or children.

I know, I know, some of you may be indignant over the man's rights, but the reality is the 96 percent to 98 percent of perpetrators of domestic violence are men. That's why I focus on the women and children as the main victims within this book. The one thing happening that gives me hope is the groups and therapists helping the men who engage in domestic violence. They encourage them to rethink their behavior and aid them in taking control of their lives to stop it because it's their problem. Until this happens on a larger scale, domestic violence will continue generation after generation.

I'm writing this book in the hopes it will open the public's eyes and minds to this crime. I use the word "crime" intentionally because that's what it is. Domestic violence has been swept under the rug, so to speak, because we have been encouraged to mind our own business and stay out of other people's.

But I think it's high time to bring this ugliness out into the open. We must stop allowing this insidious behavior to be treated as if it's just another common issue, just another woman viciously attacked and killed, just another child abused because she/he got in the way.

When it is reported in mind-numbing repetition on the nightly news, we should be standing up and saying "enough!" Why is this happening night after night, week after week, month after month, and year after year?

your head away because it makes you uncomfortable. We need more people to stand up and say "no more."

When the victim tells you it was her fault, you need to remind her that nothing she could do is deserving of this kind of treatment. When she says she doesn't want her children growing up without their daddy, remind her that seeing her abuse is teaching them the wrong way to be a family, and that it will impact them the rest of their lives even if the darkness and crime never physically touches them. When she says "I can't afford to raise my children by myself," let her know she's not alone—that there are plenty of people and organizations out there happy to assist her and are just waiting for her call.

I encourage you to consider the power of your individual choice—to remain the same and keep the cycle alive and growing or reconsider how you choose to live your life now and how that will impact others.

And I hope this book will empower you to spread the word.

"Life can only be understood backwards;
But it must be lived forwards."

-Soren Kierkegaard

Chapter One

Beginnings

I was born on a cool January afternoon in 1945 in Inglewood, a city in Los Angeles County, California. I entered this world fighting mad. My grandma told me I cried and screamed and thrashed about so much it took the doctor several minutes to determine whether I was a boy or a girl.

I was petite, barely six pounds, crowned with a mass of curly black hair and deep blue eyes. My hair went through a series of changes in my first six months but finally settled on golden blonde.

Mom and I lived with her mother and father in a guest house. My great-grandmother, who I dubbed GG, lived off the ice wagon.

When I was about two, we moved into a bigger house—white clapboard with three bedrooms, two bathrooms, and three porches. It was on a corner lot, so Grandpa had plenty of room to garden.

He planted an apricot tree that I loved to climb. I sat in the branches, plucking the tree-ripened fruit and gorging myself every summer. He planted a mixture of edibles and flowers, and the backyard was enclosed with a white picket fence; it was my playground. I loved rolling in the grass and walking barefoot on the soft moss in the borders. I especially loved swinging on the rope swing with its board seat suspended from a sturdy branch of the huge pepper tree in the center of the yard.

Grandpa loved his plants. He would come home from a day of welding at Standard Oil in El Segundo, change his clothes, and go out to water his vegetables and flowers in the yard.

The flowers surrounded the house, and I loved to go with him and silently watch his big hands spray the water over the beds his plants lived in. I learned the names of them and loved putting my hands in the earth to plant or harvest, inhaling the rich smell of the soil as it was turned. He grew herbs for Grandma's cooking and rhubarb and apricots for her pies or pandowdy, a dessert with fruit on the bottom and a cake-like topping sprinkled with sugar and cinnamon.

He had roses, geraniums, hydrangeas, carnations, and his prize-winning fuchsias that hung in baskets on the side porch and grew along the back fence.

After supper, he would relax in his easy chair and listen to the radio for a while with me on his lap. Sometimes, he fell asleep, and I would get off his lap and comb his hair. My grandpa had the most beautiful hair I've ever seen—silver-white—and I used to pray that God would change my hair to be the same color.

When I was a little older, I would stand behind his chair and put his hair up in pin curls. He would laugh at my silliness and grab me and swing me high in the air. Sometimes, he would read to me. *Beauty the Orphan Fawn,* was my favorite story that was from one of the schoolbooks Mommy brought home. He read it to me so often I memorized it. So, when he said he was too tired to read, I would hold the book and recite the story to him instead.

One day, he came home with a puppy I named JoJo. She was my constant companion until I was sixteen. She was a little, light-grey terrier mix with a stump of a tail. I taught her to climb up the stairs on my backyard slide and go down the slide with me.

Every day, the ice cream truck came down the street and grandma would give me a nickel so I could get an ice cream bar. Then I'd sit on the old swing in the backyard where I took a lick then I gave JoJo a lick. It only seemed fair since when I gave her a dog biscuit, she got a bite then I took a bite

Mom told me that I loved to color—that I would draw a picture then tell her a story about it. She said she wrote the stories down on the back of each picture, but they were lost in time, and I haven't found any of them to this day.

When I was five and a half, mom and I moved to a small community in the Mojave Desert, and that's where mom met and married a nice man who would become the only dad I ever knew. I eventually had two brothers, and we grew up in Newberry Springs.

I had a nearly idyllic childhood. The three families of mom and dad, Aunt Lillian and Uncle Abbot, and Aunt Elizabeth and Uncle John all lived on one ranch together. There were cows, chickens, pigs, ducks, and geese. I had lots of cousins to play with, and I got my first horse, Silver, for Christmas, right before my sixth birthday. He was pure white, and I named him after The Lone Ranger's horse. I got a cowgirl outfit of blue denim with white leather fringe that I put on. Once daddy lifted me up onto his back, I rode all day. When I slid off, I could barely stand up because my legs almost stuck straight out from riding, stretched in an unnatural position.

My parents only allowed me to ride him bareback because when one of the girls across the highway was riding her horse thru the lava beds, she fell off, and her foot was caught in the stirrup. It spooked her horse, and it ran home, terrified. It dragged her as she dangled upside down, causing a severe head injury.

day, I came home from school to find Sirloin missing. When I ran to mom to ask her where he went, she replied, "He went to the butcher." I was devasted. It got worse! When beef started showing up in our meals, I asked if this was Sirloin. When mom said yes, I choked and threw up. I didn't eat beef for years after that.

Mom was the principal of my elementary school as well as my teacher. Not an ideal situation for me. She was harder on me than the other kids because I had the advantage of preschool *and* kindergarten. The other kids were just starting school for the first time. I also had to remember to call her "teacher" while we were at school. It was all very confusing. She told me it was so the other kids wouldn't call me teacher's pet, but between my preschool and the fact that they knew she was my mother, I got teased a lot anyway.

I was quiet and shy but did manage to make a couple of friends. There were times I was teased unmercifully, as we have all heard children are so mean, yet, I not only endured the teasing, but survived. I believe that experience had me always sticking up for the underdog. I think it also primed me to stick it out when facing adversity.

Just a few years ago, I got a message through the Classmates app from a guy from my primary school days. He told me that after all these years, he remembered being new to the school. On the day his father had passed away, he sat crying alone, and I took the time to sit and talk with him. He wanted to reach out to thank me for that simple kindness. You never know when something you do or

Beyond Surviving •

19

to that small, lonely boy.

I went to Barstow for high school and joined the marching band and acapella choir. I was in the Girls Athletic Association and excelled on the trampoline. I was also in the Junior class play "Saved by The Belle." We had one dressing room for both the boys and girls. One night, during a costume change, the boys refused to leave so I told them that I had to change and, if they wouldn't leave, I would just have to change in front of them. That was pretty bold for the 1950s. I turned my back to them and started to take off my blouse. They left in a big hurry. I don't know what I would have done if they stayed, but I called their bluff.

Every Wednesday night I stayed in town with my best friend, Susan; her mom was the organist at our church and Wednesday was when we had choir practice. Susan and I always went to the A&W drive-in for a root beer float after dinner but before practice. It was where the kids from school hung out. I wasn't really part of the "cool" kids because I lived so far out of town, but that one night a week I really felt like I belonged. I graduated third in my class and eagerly looked forward to attending college.

Attending UCLA in the early 60s was a whole different world for me. I lived in the only all-women's dorm on campus, Myra Hershey Hall, located across the street from the sorority houses and right at the edge of the Botanical Gardens. Mom took me to the Admissions office and signed all the enrollment papers. Suddenly, I was on my own for the first time in my life. I made up my mind I was not going to be that shy girl anymore. After all, there were thousands

I joined the rally committee; went to on-campus concerts; joined the fencing club—I even won a trophy playing badminton. I made friends and went on a few dates. My major was economics with a minor in history. The economics was my "practical" choice and history was my "interest" choice. I was fascinated by anthropology, but at that time I could never have gone on a live dig, so I just learned what I could and enjoyed myself.

One of the newly formed Kennedy Administration's Peace Corps groups came to our dorm for meals. Listening to their discussions around the table opened a whole new world of possibilities in my mind. I fantasized about joining the Peace Corp after I graduated, but realistically I knew that I was expected to follow the path my mom had laid out for me long ago—I was to go to college, get a job, get married, and have children. This was the accepted pathway for women at that time. More women were entering the workforce, but their main expectation was to get married and set up housekeeping and support their husband's work. After college, I shared an apartment with two girlfriends from my college dorm. The apartment was in West Los Angeles and had two bedrooms, two baths, a dining area, living room, and kitchen. They each had a bedroom and I slept on the couch. It was my first experience living with a couple of girlfriends off campus. I loved the freedom of eating what and when I wanted, listening to my music, and reading whatever I was interested in at the time. I have always had a love affair with books and continue to learn something new as often as the opportunity presents itself.

next door. He said good morning twice before I could find my voice to answer and gave me a smile. Looking back, it was more an Elvis-like sneer, but then he headed off to work. I was mesmerized. He was tall and had a style that was part clown and part sexy bad-boy.

We said good morning regularly from that day on, and, one day, he asked me up for a coke. We gradually fell into short conversations where we were getting acquainted.

He worked out back in his parking space on his car in the evenings and weekends, and he eventually asked me to keep him company. I would sit and chat away, occasionally handing him a tool. Dad had been an auto mechanic when mom and I met him, so I knew a bit about car engines and the various tools required to work on them. When he got it running, he took me out for a ride. There was no floor-board, so it was both exhilarating and terrifying to look down and watch the blacktop speed past. I couldn't believe my good fortune. Me, from a little desert community, stumbling across someone so cool who liked me? It almost felt like a fairytale come true.

Michael and his roommate had a crow named Joe they rescued and kept in a makeshift cage in their apartment, and Mike was teaching himself to play the guitar. In fact, he cut a demo record with some friends, but it never went anywhere.

I thought we were a couple. My mom and grandma had come over for dinner and I forgot something at the store. Michael volunteered to go pick it up for me. When it seemed behind my apartment, making out with my roommate. I was crushed, but he convinced me it was no big deal to him, and soon we went back to the way we were before. It should have been a red flag. If this was no big deal, why did he do it? And why would I believe I was a big deal to him after finding him with my roommate?

There were two girls who lived next door to him and the four of us became fast friends. We partied together, played together, ran around together, and generally had lots of fun. We were close to Santa Monica Beach, so we hung out there a lot. It was the early 60s. Life was an exciting new adventure.

We started going to my parents at least once a month. My family really liked him; he was intelligent and funny and, as a bonus, he liked to play cards. I thought life couldn't get much better. I had finished college, was employed at the Security Pacific Bank in the heart of Beverly Hills, and, most importantly, I had a boyfriend. I could check off the first two items on the life-list and was on the fast-track to on the third.

The first time he said "I love you," to me, we were at the beach, and he brought along a couple of champagne glasses and a bottle of nice champagne for a toast. It was so romantic. But, he wasn't ready for marriage. When we spoke about it, his go-to comment was he wasn't going to be "pussy-whipped." Mom and Dad didn't help much by constantly hinting about grandchildren.

One day, right before Christmas, I passed out at work, and when I came to, one of the managers at the bank called kidney infection. He put me on a clear liquid diet for two weeks. We went back to my apartment to pick up some clothes before they took me to back to Newberry to spend a month recuperating. I was so angry; I felt they were treating me like a child.

Michael was there waiting for us. I told him when I called to tell him the results of the doctor's appointment that my parents were going to take me back with them to the desert. He kicked in the door to his apartment which, looking back, should have been another clue to his violent behavior but at the time I thought was terribly romantic. He was in such a great hurry to get inside so he could give me my Christmas present before I had to leave with Mom and Dad. It was a beautiful baby blue straight skirt and an angora blue and white sweater. I didn't even get a chance to try it on and show him because my parents were so anxious to get home. He told me he loved me and that I would be fine. And he said he would stop and see me on his way back to Wisconsin.

He went home to his mom in Wisconsin for Christmas and New Year's Day. That's when he decided to go back to school at the University of Wisconsin in Madison to complete his degree. It was a very long year, as far as I was concerned. I wrote lots of letters and we talked on the phone almost daily, but long-distance calling was expensive. There were many unexplained absences when I called, and I often ended up falling asleep with his phone still ringing. It seemed he was busy doing more than studying for his degree, but I pushed it out of my mind.

Company of North America. My roommates had returned to school for their Masters degrees, Michael moved back in with his old roommate, and I found a single apartment for me and my cat.

We fell into the habit of spending Christmas Eve with his mom and sister after they moved to California, then we'd drive for two hours to spend Christmas Day with my parents. As I opened my present from him our fourth Christmas together, I was stupefied. It was a carburetor for my car. Then he told me to look inside, and there was a beautiful diamond solitaire ring.

I would have liked a small wedding with Dad walking me down the aisle, but he was adamant there would be no religious ceremony. It took four years for him to even get to asking me to marry him and made it clear that, if I wanted to marry him, it would be his way.

Three weeks later as we drove to Las Vegas to get married, I asked him to stop and pick up Mom and Dad so they could be there, but he didn't want to take the time. It seemed that once he decided to "take the plunge" he didn't want to wait. On the way home, we stopped to tell my parents that we had gotten married, but they weren't home, and I ended up just leaving a note. When we got home, we made our first purchase—a bed. We rented a two-story apartment on the second and third floors of a building in Santa Monica, north of Wilshire Blvd., and spent the better part of a week moving in. That was my honeymoon.

because he didn't want it to infringe on his freedom. He started going out with his buddies from work at least once or twice a week, and when I complained, he said, "I can do what I want. I told you before we got married that I wouldn't be tied down." Then he started going fishing with his best friend for the weekend. I was lonely and couldn't understand why he preferred spending so much time with his buddies instead of spending his time with me. So, to distract myself, I started shopping and doing things with my new friends from work.

Then Michael bought a pool table so he and his friends could drink and have something to do in the house. At least he was home a little more. He continued to go out drinking with his work friends at least two nights a week, getting home between 3:30 and 6:45 in the morning. He also started accusing me of seeing another man when he wasn't around. I think that was pure projection on his part because he was spending time with other women. His fishing trips continued about once a month, and I had a lot of lonely weekends. I joined a bowling team and occasionally went to the movies or somewhere with my girlfriends from work.

Our vacations over the years consisted of great camping trips. We saw some beautiful country. We slept in sleeping bags by the ocean or hiked into the backcountry with a mule in Yosemite—always a place where he could fish, and I could hike or read. We never left California, but I loved the peacefulness of where we went. He would get angry because I wasn't interested in fishing. He didn't want to eat the fish, and I couldn't think of killing something for insisted on taking along one of his guns "for protection." It made me nervous because I don't like guns, but I allowed it since it seemed to make him feel better.

Once, at Shasta Lake, he caught a stringer of fish and left them in the water overnight so he could take pictures the next morning. Unfortunately, turtles had found the helpless fish and ate their gills so they drowned. He was mad that he'd missed his photoshoot, and I was sobbing thinking about the poor fish who couldn't get away from the predation, which made him even madder. "They're only fish," he yelled, "so shut up!"

Another vacation I told him I was pregnant. Instead of being happy and excited, he told me to "get rid of it" because we were in no position to have a baby. I spent a good deal of that vacation crying. I had waited to tell him until we were away from the city, in hopes he would be less stressed and in a more receptive mood. So much for that plan. When we got home, he arranged for me to get an abortion.

I am not, in principle, opposed to the procedure, but it didn't mean I wanted one. My choice was to keep the baby, but he made it clear that he would either leave, or I could abort the fetus and he would stay. Not strong enough to make it on my own, I made the wrong choice and had the abortion. I remember hearing a woman in the operating room crying and pleading, "please don't take my baby". I was devastated and felt trapped into a decision I didn't want but I couldn't face life without Michael.

based on how my body reacted when I was pregnant with my son. We also had a house by then, and I was afraid I would lose the house which my Grandma had loaned us the money for a down payment, as well as losing my husband. I've learned that life is a series of choices, and the ones we make determine where we go from there. I've also learned that objects are what we focus on, but it's life itself that's important.

Two years after the abortion, my son was born. Mike still wasn't happy about having a baby around but felt "it was time." Ward was such a sweet, happy little guy and I thought, like so many other women, that he would bring us close again. Mike seemed to adore him and bragged about "his" son all the time. But he was jealous that I was breastfeeding because he was very attached to my breasts and considered them his personal property. He was also resentful of all the time I spent with the baby.

I was exhausted after returning to work after my maternity leave, and it seemed like all Mike wanted was sex. He complained when I wasn't "into it." I felt more and more depressed and distant from him. He next decided he needed to quit his job so he could "find himself"—I became our sole financial supporter, as well as taking care of a new baby, and scared I couldn't do it all by myself.

My boss at work was attentive and supportive. He invited me to lunch so we could talk away from the office. Gradually, I was feeling more accepted by him because he was so understanding about my feelings and how much pressure I felt I was under. I was torn between my feelings for both pressure on me, was telling me quite frequently how inadequate I was. I wasn't a good housekeeper, I wasn't sexy anymore, I came home from work tired and only had the energy to take care of the baby and fix dinner. I compared this to my boss who seemingly appreciated me just the way I was.

At this point, I was tired of being accused of seeing other men for years, when I knew he had at least two other women he saw on a pretty regular basis. I was leaning more and more toward leaving Michael and thought that if I was being accused, I might as well get the satisfaction of actually doing it. My time with my boss morphed into dinner, then into a series of afternoon delights. As it turned out, the old saying "two wrong things don't make a right" is true for a reason. Yet another bad choice on my part.

It was then I thought I was strong enough to leave my marriage, so I told Mike I was leaving him. He demanded to know who I was going to leave with, believing I wasn't strong enough to leave him on my own. And that was the beginning of the end. He stormed out of the house to "talk" with Bob. It got ugly really fast from there.

"One of the hardest lessons in life is letting go. Whether it's guilt, anger, love, loss or betrayal. Change is never easy. We fight to hold on and we fight to let go."

-8-Images.Blogspot.com

Chapter Two

A Living Nightmare

I never heard my parents fight over anything. When they disagreed, they talked things over like the adults they were. So, when my marriage turned bad, I had no idea what was happening. I drifted along for almost three years trying to keep my head above water in the relationship. I felt guilty for having an affair with my boss even though Mike had numerous affairs and/or one-night stands throughout our marriage. I also felt guilty thinking about taking Ward away from his father, because Mike's dad died when he was four and his mother never remarried. Growing up without a father had a devastating effect on Mike.

effect on Ward. He started out as a happy little guy but turned into a bully (then an abuser) himself. The lesson I learned too late was that staying in that kind of relationship for the sake of children is not the best reason. My son learned not only to be afraid of other people being able to hurt him but became a bully as a result of that fear. Ward was not only tall, but he was very strong. Because of his size, it was easy to intimidate others around him, so he was protected by their fear of him.

Once, when he was about twelve, he came and asked me for money to buy candy at the store. I told him no. He picked me up, pinned my arms to my sides, and threatened to hold me there until I gave in to his wishes. I reminded him that he would get tired, and he might as well put me down, and that my answer wasn't going to change. He gave in after about a minute and never tried this tactic on me again—but the experience was disconcerting. He began running away from home shortly after that incident. I realize now that he was running away from an atmosphere that he couldn't control. Due to his early experiences, he thought that unless he was in total control, he could be hurt.

It was a Tuesday morning, and I could hear Ward playing in his room. Time to get ready for the next chapter in our lives. His preschool was starting in an hour, and I had a lot to get done before we left. I had planned it all out the day before while I was meticulously cleaning the house, so my husband would have nothing to complain about. I even cleaned the tile grout in the kitchen with a toothbrush.

mined to leave behind the pain and humiliation Mike inflicted on me. In the last three years, I had endured so much abuse at Michael's hand: beatings, strangling, raping me vaginally and anally with a gun, hitting my head on the bathroom counter until I passed out, kicking me in the belly when I was pregnant, urinating on me, and stripping me and locking me outside in a cold rain. The torture also included threatening to kill me if I ever left, threatening to take my son away so I would never see him again, killing the dog in front of me then turning the gun on me while saying, "I can do it, I can do it ."

More abuse consisted of keeping a gun under his side of the mattress, leaving me at Toys R Us on Christmas Eve then, when I got home, accusing me of taking my time to go "fuck" someone because he had come back to get me and didn't see me. Once he actually reached inside my body and tried to rip out my vagina. He subjected me to daily verbal and emotional abuse, telling me repeatedly that I was nothing but a stupid bitch.

He also put an external lock on my son's bedroom and would lock him in while all this was going on. Ward would pound on the door crying to let him out, to stop hurting his mom, and Michael would tell him to shut up that I deserved it. I also caught him trying to teach my 2-year-old son to say "Mama's a whore" while he was smiling, as if he were teaching him a game. It was chilling to see.

After reading the last few paragraphs, you must be wondering why I stayed. What most people don't understand about being in this kind of abusive relationship is that the life was righting itself—that the abuse was an anomaly, not the other way around.

We'd take Ward to the pony rides or drive to the beach for a picnic. It's called the honeymoon phase in the cycle of violence. Most women are isolated from family and friends, and their only adult contact is the abuser. It skews their reality and makes the victim totally dependent on the abuser. It's almost like being a prisoner of war, but even there you have other prisoners to talk with. How many of you have seen movies where the warden or commandant keeps a prisoner in isolation and abuses him?

It wouldn't be the first time I left, but I was determined it would be my last. Statistically, I later learned, women leave their abusers four to six times before they leave for good. I'd gone to two different friends and to my parents a couple of times, yet Mike always found me and convinced me to come home again. Begging me and assuring me that he loved me.

Once, my dad drove me from Arizona to LA to file for divorce. I couldn't believe how beautiful the carpet of wild-flowers was along the side of the road and stretching into the distance. It seemed the entire desert was celebrating spring while I was in the midst of feeling like my life had ended. It felt like nature was rubbing my nose in it.

Michael followed me to Mom and Dad's and begged me to come home. He had even started seeing a counselor who I talked to before I was willing to go back. My parents encouraged me to return and try again to work it out. I hadn't

The first few days were like walking on eggshells. I made an appointment to see the counselor, but Michael insisted on going with me. The therapist told me I was lucky to have Michael, that he'd rarely seen a patient who could express his feelings so well. I simply agreed to continue to see him. Then, the divorce papers arrived and were served. All hell broke loose!

Just to stay safe, I signed a quit claim deed to my share of the house. When my husband left to go for a drive to see his girlfriend and took Ward with him, I called the therapist and told him I couldn't see him with Michael present anymore. If he wanted to continue talking to me, it had to be alone. After hearing what I had to say, he agreed. At our next joint session, he told Michael that he needed to see us separately for a while because the joint sessions weren't going anywhere.

When I had been beaten the night before our next session, the counselor was genuinely surprised since his experience with Michael was so positive. A couple of sessions later, there had been more abuse. He told me that if I told him about anymore that he would have to report it to the police. I remembered the last time the police came—when I was sent to the bathroom to clean up my face—before letting them see me. As I was approaching the living room, I heard Michael tell them that he hadn't hurt me but that if he did, I deserved it, and they were all chuckling about it. So, I certainly didn't feel safe telling them what had happened that night.

was nothing I could do about it; he had cut off all my exits.

In the end, it was humiliation that sent me fleeing. The proverbial straw that broke the camel's back was when Michael ordered me to go get him cigarettes two nights before, wearing only a mini dress, no bra, and no under-pants. He knew I wouldn't be able to get the cigarettes without exposing myself, and he thought it would be funny knowing I would be really embarrassed. Then, when I got back, he was furious that I went out dressed like that, even though it was his idea, and the night deteriorated from there.

I carefully packed my clothes and Ward's clothes in a king-sized pillowcase. I couldn't risk my husband finding a packed suitcase, and this was the best thing I could think of to hold enough for both me and Ward. I put it and Ward's bike into the car, fixed us some breakfast, and we were gone.

It felt surreal driving away from the house, knowing it would be for the last time. As I watched in the rearview mirror while we pulled away from the house, I felt like the terror my life had become was getting smaller and smaller, behind me at last. When I turned the corner, the house was no longer in sight. I took a deep breath and drove out of that life and into a new beginning.

"Remember, no one can make you feel inferior without your consent."

-Eleanor Roosevelt

Chapter Three

Safe Haven

Driving down the freeway, I watched the rearview mirror to be sure Michael wasn't following me. "Please God, don't let that happen," I prayed. I didn't know what I'd do if we didn't get away.

I got off the freeway, pulled over to check my directions, and made sure I hadn't been followed. It was only a few miles down the street, and we were there. At first glance, it looked to me like a group of old-fashioned vacation cabins instead of a shelter for battered women. Taking a deep breath, I stepped out of the car with my four-year-old son, walked up the three steps from the sidewalk to the entrance, opened the wooden gate in the picket fence, and each cement walk that ran in front of the cabins. There was a playground area at the rear of the property and a building set up like a preschool,, fully equipped with the tools and toys of children at the end of the walkway.

I opened the door and walked into what I hoped would be the start of our new lives and introduced myself. A staff woman took me into a room off to the side to do an intake, while another took Ward out to the playground. She offered me a drink of water and began the interview. I thought it was to determine whether I was suitable for their shelter but later found out it was really to determine how much abuse I had suffered at the hands of my husband, how much he drank, and to rate his level of violence. Only much later did I learn that he was rated the most dangerous on their scale—a ten on a scale of one to ten.

They went over the rules, and I signed a contract with the facility. Another woman went to my car with me and helped me bring in the meager belongings I had packed for us to start over. It's funny how narrow your focus gets when you're dealing with life and death choices. Everything I brought had a purpose and, of course, had to fit into one king-sized pillowcase with the exception of Ward's bike. I couldn't force myself to make him leave everything behind, even though I had no problem doing so with my own possessions. To me they were just things and things can be replaced.

We were assigned to a cabin that we were to share with another woman and her little girl. The living room was furnished with two easy chairs and side tables, a love seat with to the right, furnished with cooking and eating utensils and an oval wooden table with six ladder-backed chairs. Two bedrooms were down a hall to the left off the living room and had bunk beds, a small wooden chest of drawers, and closet in each one. There was also a common bathroom that had a tub and shower, a small sink in a vanity with a mirror, and a small cupboard with towels, washcloths, soap, toothbrushes, and toothpaste.

I was lucky my son was only four because they didn't take male children over six due to the possibility of learned violence. I would never have gone in if they hadn't allowed Ward—there was no way I would leave him with his father.

I put away our few clothes, more of my son's than mine, and looked around. It was interesting to me that I felt more comfortable here in a small cabin than in my own house. For the first time in years, I felt safe.

My cabinmate kept to herself most of the time, but we gradually started to share our experiences. Though the individual experiences were different, they had a common denominator—Experiencing suffering abuse at the hands of our husbands and feeling trapped. Because of this, she and I kept in touch for years after moving on to our separate lives. The last time I heard from her she was back in Shreveport with her daughter and making a new life for herself. It was an eyeopener for me to find that I wasn't even close to being the only one who's life had become a living hell.

premises for three days. Most women who return to their homes do so in that length of time. Cell phones didn't exist then and there were no phones in the cabins so that no one would be tempted to contact their abuser. I was allowed to call my parents and let them know I was safe, as well as my friend who gave me the number to this shelter.

When I was given permission to leave the grounds, the first place I went to was the library. I checked out a book about anger. I still wanted to help Mike, and thought if I understood him, I could make it okay to go home. The counselor I was assigned to spent the first week of daily sessions telling me that what he had been doing was a common pattern abusers use, and it wasn't my fault. I was still stuck in "if I hadn't done (fill in the blank), he wouldn't have hurt me" and worrying about how he was handling us being gone.

It took a long time for me to realize that the abuse was his choice of reaction to his pain, not anything I had done, and it was certainly not my fault. He was using physical and emotional abuse to control and punish me because he was in emotional pain. *Nothing* I had done warranted physical abuse. I told her that after years of being accused, and years of him going out with other women, I had an affair. She enlightened me by saying he had many options: he could have left, divorced me, or talked it through with me and we might have worked it out, or we could have gotten separated, yet the one he chose was violence and repeatedly attacking me.

angry. Since I rarely turned to anger, I really didn't understand it. So, in reading the book to help him, I instead found answers that helped me. I also learned that there are many other ways to deal with rage than striking out at others. A bully is really just someone bigger than others who uses their strength to intimidate people while covering up their own fear.

We all had to go to Social Services and apply for food stamps and welfare. This was a humiliating task for me, even though it was totally necessary. I thought only really poor people had to resort to these services, and I had never considered myself part of that category. I was rather quickly disabused of that prejudicial notion. How else could I feed my son and myself, both at the shelter and after we moved out, without this meager supplement? I got the food stamps immediately and was able to go to the grocery store for the first time since I left home. It felt wonderful to do something so simple and normal again.

We had daily counseling, both personal and group. In the group sessions, I was introduced to creative visualization. Wikipedia defines creative visualization as "the cognitive process of purposefully generating visual mental imagery, with intent to experience a subsequent beneficial physiological, psychological or social effect.," Being very visual myself, I embraced it with open arms and later became a Master of Therapeutic Imagery, creative visualization, to use in conjunction with hypnosis to help people resolve emotional bruises. It takes you anywhere you want to go and is a wonderful stress reliever.

clothes that I wore for years because they were so nice. Ward was growing so fast I was lucky to find clothes that fit him. This saved me the expense of having to buy clothes for going on job interviews and for Ward to wear to school.

We were required to attend Al-Anon Meetings for the partners of alcoholics because the shelter's funding source was tied to alcohol abuse. They introduced me to the concept of codependence, but I refused to accept that I was in any way at fault for his abusive behavior, so I opted to provide childcare for the rest of the meetings. In my mind, if it was his choice to abuse me, then I wasn't codependent, and it wasn't my choice for him to drink himself into being unconscious or out of control. In fact, I would have preferred he not drink, because that's when his abuse really escalated.

The shelter helped me understand that he wasn't abusive because of the alcohol he drank; he just found it easier to abuse me when drinking because his inhibitions were lowered. That was a powerful lesson for me. It wasn't the alcohol or drugs; the darkness was in him all along and was ultimately his choice. Unfortunately, he drank a bottle of Crown Royal a day which facilitated access to his inner demons. To this day I can't stand even the smell of whisky.

The children's program director was wonderful and taught me so many helpful lessons about child rearing without physical punishment. I grew up in the country and spankings were an acceptable way of correcting unacceptable behavior in a child. Not that I was big on spanking, but my son was big for his age, and I was less than 100 tank pushing me around. We all had to take primary care of our children, but there were programs designed to help the kids with their problems arising from being in abusive home environments. I was really grateful for this help.

I do have to mention that some of the new ways of working to change unhealthy behavior don't seem to work with every child. Whether that child is damaged beyond control or so smart they can out-maneuver the parent, I don't know, but what I do know is that my son managed to manipulate the therapists I took him to. They were supposed to help him learn better ways to navigate life, but instead he crawled around on the floor playing with toys while telling them he didn't have to talk about life around his dad. Two different therapists told me there was nothing they could do for him. I was on my own as far as raising Ward and dealing with his issues.

We needed to find a place to move when our month was up at the shelter, and I needed a job. We had to find schooling and/or childcare for our children once we were on our own. It was a crash course on jump starting a new life, and though it was exhausting, it was exhilarating at the same time. I would finally be in charge of my destiny!

In between all the assignments we had, the women at the shelter still took the time to get to know one another and share our stories. We'd go to the grocery store together, walk around the neighborhood, or just gather in each other's cabins to share our frustrations and successes. Having a car to help the others run errands helped me feel like I was giving back to the community of women as well as do what

The shelter arranged an outing for all of us to attend at the Comedy Club in Hollywood, on Women's Night. We learned to laugh again which, in itself, was very healing. Halloween came and we took our kids to trick-or-treat around the neighborhood in a group, then dealt with the sugar highs together.

It was a special time in my life and helped prepare me to face life on my own terms. I stayed in touch with several of the women I met there for a long time after we all left. We had the bond of common experience that crossed all other lines. Domestic violence is colorblind and does not discriminate against age, gender or economic circumstances. Knowing that Mike had been an insurance investigator I was continually concerned with him finding us.

"Every day is a chance to begin again. Don't focus on the failures of yesterday, start today with positive thoughts and expectations."

-Catherine Pulsifer

Chapter Four

Starting Over

It took several attempts to find a job locally that would pay enough to support us and allow me to afford preschool for Ward. I went on numerous interviews thinking that my previous experience would make finding a good job relatively easy, but I hadn't taken into consideration that having been unemployed for four years would be an obstacle. Even with excellent references, it was something I had to overcome.

Remember, it was in the early '80s, and having a young child was still a hindrance to hiring women. There were questions that are no longer allowed in an interview today but were normal back then like: "Why was there such denly because of my husband finding us?" "Will you quit again to take care of another child if you get pregnant?" But I persevered and found a great job as a staff accountant at United Geophysical right in the town I was to call home. I found a nice preschool for Ward and set a starting date for my new job. My new life was beginning to take shape.

Next, I needed to find a place to live outside the shelter. I wasn't interested in an apartment like my other friends. I wanted to see if I could find a house I could afford. I hit the jackpot, so to speak, when I found a guest house behind a large main house on Huntington Blvd. in South Pasadena. It was perfect for me and Ward, with a large family kitchen, decent sized living room, two bedrooms and a shared bath which, to my delight, contained a clawfoot bathtub with a shower attachment.

It was hard to say goodbye to the women and staff at the shelter that had been my refuge for the past month. I felt both safe and validated there and being alone with Ward was, at the same time, exciting and terrifying, but it was time for us to move forward.

The next challenge was to get everything it takes to make a house habitable. I had so much fun going to estate sales and used furniture stores—it was like being on a scavenger hunt. My great aunt had been storing the furniture of her recently deceased sister, and all I had to do was pick it up. Mom and Dad came down to help me move the furniture and get everything set up. Mom took me to Target to get essentials, dishes, bathroom necessities, pots and pans,

It was like moving into my own fairytale home with white clapboard, front and back porches, and a tiny backyard, plus my own one-car garage. I took my counselor by to look at and approve it before I could move in, which she was happy to do. I negotiated the rent down to my comfort zone. By the time I got what I needed to make the house livable, I felt right at home. It was eclectic and practically nothing matched, but everything reflected my taste and it suited me to a T.

The morning I was to start my job, Ward woke up with a fever. *Great,* I thought, *this is the perfect way to start something new!* But my little boy was sick. I called Human Resources (HR) at my new placement to tell them I couldn't start that day and why. They were very understanding and told me to let them know when I could be there and to take as long as I needed to make sure my son was okay. I felt like angels were watching over me to have found a place so understanding.

He'd been fine the day before, but his fever was so high it scared me. I took Ward to the doctor and found out he had pneumonia. I was stunned. The doctor gave him a shot and told me to take him home and get his fever down. If I couldn't manage that, he would have to be hospitalized. Even with a job, I had no health insurance, so for three days I bathed him with cool wash cloths and gave him popsicles and water or juice. I called Mom and Dad again, and they came down to stay with him so I could get started at work. I was so lucky to have their support. They came all the way from Arizona when I needed help.

I was plagued with self-doubt. What if I couldn't do what was needed? What if they didn't like me? But again, my guardian angels were there to assure me that I had this. My supervisor was a young woman who couldn't have been kinder getting me settled in and got me started with bank reconciliations, which I could do with my eyes closed. At lunch break, I met a couple of my coworkers. They worked in the foreign accounting division, and they were as curious about me as I was about them That was the beginning a lifelong friendship with one of them. I gave a sigh of relief, and I stepped into my new life.

Ward recovered and went back to preschool, Mom and Dad went back to Arizona, and I fell into the new pattern of my life as a single parent. I have to say that even though my life was simpler, it was hard to adjust to living a regular way of life after spending three years living on a rollercoaster of emotion.

I think that there's something almost addictive about the cycle of violence. The emotions are so exaggerated most of the time, it's strange to not have them anymore. My "normal" had changed from just surviving to simply living, and I needed time to settle into it. And I think I was probably depressed. I was exhausted all of the time. I wasn't used to having the sole responsibility of another person's life as well as my own. Working and paying bills were just normal stuff I'd done all my adult life, but now there was the added weight of figuring out how best to care for Ward and where I wanted to go from there.

His life had gone from two parents who loved him, all while his father yelled and struck at me in too many ways to count, to me struggling to survive while taking care of him and making his life as normal as I was able.

As I stated earlier, Michael had put a lock on the outside of Ward's bedroom door. When he was going to "start" in on me, he locked my son in his room, leaving him crying and pounding on the door while yelling, "Stop talking to my mom that way!" or "You're scaring me!", or "You're hurting my mom! Stop it!" Ward was very verbal by the time he was two and really sensitive. So, he learned very early in his life that he was powerless against his dad—but he also learned how to manipulate people, women in particular.

At night, alone with no one to talk to, I could relax and listen to music while I read a good book. I rarely read novels at that point in my life. I preferred to read self-help books, ones that would help me grow past the fears that held me back, and books that helped me realize that I could pull myself together and appreciate who I was becoming. I needed to hear that I was stronger, more self-reliant, confidant, and that I had done the right thing. I escaped a living nightmare of constant physical and emotional abuse and was building a nonviolent life for me and my son.

While there had been emotional abuse all along, it was a zing here or a zap there that slowly eroded my belief in myself. Mike was always looking at other women and commenting about how beautiful they were or how sexy they looked. As are many abusers, he was very charismatic, and

I did have. And he fed on that.

He started telling me how to dress, then berating me when other men looked my way. He would tell me what to wear when we went to a party of his friends, who to talk to, and what I could and couldn't say. He ended up at a point where he told me I would be nothing if he hadn't taught me how to be, and that I had made him a wife beater. I finally reminded him that I never brought his hand down on me or gave him all the inventive ways he came up with to abuse me.

But I digress. My life was back on a more normal track. I had friends. I didn't have to ask anyone for permission to do anything I wanted to do or ask for money, and my life with Ward was becoming more normal. I was no longer scared of being at home, and Ward picked up on that. He wanted a kitten, so I looked around and found a cute little tabby he promptly named Peter for Peter Cottontail. Then we added a grey calico we named Einstein. So, we each had a pet.

We had picnics with friends, and we went to the movies and shopping. We went to museums and public gardens on weekends like the Arboretum. I got to buy clothes that were my taste and even bought a couple of suits for work. I also started building credit in my name only. Ward made a wonderful friend in school, TJ, The two took turns staying at each other's house. His mom picked them both up from school and took them home with her when I started working a new job outside of Pasadena.

along with a pot of tomatoes and one of strawberries. It was finally turning into a home for us instead of just a house I rented.

There was a grade school just down the street where Ward could go when he graduated from preschool. In the evening after dinner, he could roller skate on the school grounds.

I had friends to talk with or shop with. One of my new friends owned a horse and invited me to go riding after work with her occasionally. I hadn't really ridden since high school and was excited to get on a horse again. The first time out, by the time I got home, my legs were so sore that I soaked a good hour in the old clawfoot tub with some Epsom salts.

Wednesday nights I went to group counseling with the other Haven "grads" while Ward was in childcare. I felt like I was recovering well, and we supported each other through thick and thin. It gave me a link with others who had had similar experiences and kept me connected with a supportive community while I was finding my new life. It also kept what I had endured in front of me. I began to wonder how Michael was faring. The group told me to focus on Ward and me, that Michael was moving forward with his life just as I was with ours. But, knowing the abusive background he had grown up in, I wasn't so sure.

We spent holidays with my parents and brothers in the desert, and Ward got to reconnect with some of his cousins. At that time, there were lots of man-made lakes in the area where my brothers were, and we had fun taking the kids to we did when I was growing up. I could relax and know there were other adults around to keep an eye on Ward. It took me back to that feeling of community.

After the second Christmas in our own home, I took a deep breath and decided that I should let Michael know we were okay and that he could see Ward with supervised visits. He was, after all, Ward's father, and I thought he should be able to see his son. I didn't want to put Ward through the empty hole left in his life that Michael had by losing his dad so early. I picked up the receiver and made the call.

"Even though there are days I wish I could change some things in the past, there's a reason the rear-view mirror is so small and the windshield is so big, where you're headed is much more important that what you've left behind."

-Unknown

Chapter Five

One Step Forward, Two Steps Back

Michael lost his father when he was four, and I knew how he felt growing up without a dad. He was so relieved to hear from me, and though talk was a bit stilted, we did chat for quite a while. I'd kept track of him through a friend, knew he was going to AA, and allegedly hadn't had a drink since I left. Knowing that the drinking didn't cause his abusive behavior, I agreed to meet him with Ward in a public place the following week and see how it went.

Michael, I was shocked at how his appearance had changed. He'd lost a lot of weight—in fact he looked downright haggard. His hands shook. He was chain smoking. All signs that he was as nervous as I was. He spread a blanket on the grass for us to sit on close to the playground equipment, so we could keep an eye on Ward. My son kept trying to drag him off to play, but Michael just wanted to talk with me. I reminded him that we were here so he could spend time with his son. He finally relented and went to crawl around in the castle with Ward for a while.

He told me he had changed—that he was going to AA and had done a lot of soul searching. He was sorry for everything he had done to me, how it was wrong of him to hit me. He wanted us to move back home with him. I was not ready to do that and told him he had to really take this slow if there was a chance for us to resolve our differences. I needed to see that he had improved, not just listen to him tell me.

He repeated that he had been going to AA since I left and hadn't had a drink in all that time. I said I thought that was great but that the drinking itself wasn't the problem. He looked stunned, so I explained what I had learned at the shelter. I told him that alcohol wasn't the problem, it simply lowered inhibitions, so someone who was drinking didn't show much restraint. I chose my words carefully so as not use him as an example, but the implication that he belonged to that group of violent abusers was there.

Then he wanted to know where we lived and was upset when I wouldn't tell him. We ate some sandwiches and

Ward told him the name of his school, and he was able to later narrow down the area that way. He had begun working for a private detective, so he'd been looking for us for quite a while. Before we left, I had agreed for him to meet with Ward again.

It was almost New Year's Day, so we decided to go see the floats after the annual Rose Parade. They were on display in a park where they are every year for the public to view for a few days after the parade ends. We were to meet at a restaurant and go to the park together. The floats were as beautiful as they looked on TV, but Ward was frightened by the huge crowd wandering around. Being that he was only five and most attendees were adults, he couldn't see much until we were right next to a float. He felt lost in a sea of bodies. Michael didn't even offer to lift him up and put him on his shoulders. Ward started to cry. At that, Michael decided we were leaving.

After that, we only met for a meal here and there, but we talked a lot and came to some understanding. I let him take Ward for a weekend during which he seemed to take a lot of time talking to me on the phone and acknowledging how difficult being a single parent to our son would be.

Then, he wanted me to meet a woman he'd met at AA who had kids around Ward's age. I figured if I was trying for a reconciliation, it would be a good idea for Ward to have a friend or two, so I agreed. She was easy to talk to and a professional cake decorator, which I found interesting. She was getting a huge cake ready for the Country Western Music Awards, and I got to watch as she created

Livingston Seagull aloud to her when we ran out of topics to just chat about.

I listened to her problems quite a bit and heard all about how her husband was trying to take her kids from her, and how helpful Michael had been. I could tell she had a big crush on him, and I decided that weekend I would prefer to have her friendship than be with Michael romantically. It was clear that even though he'd been looking for us all the time we'd been separated that he really hadn't changed his desire for other women. It made me wonder what else hadn't really changed.

I finally let him know where we lived, and he came over fairly frequently. He would take Ward down the alley to the school at the end of the block. They could roller skate or play hide-and-seek while I fixed dinner. Then after dinner, we'd watch a little TV or talk. He was slowly becoming angry at me again and started with the accusations about other men. It was then that I told him he needed to leave.

One night, he paused at the door to yell at me that it was my fault he turned into a wife beater. I shot back that he'd managed to do that all on his own; I had never taken his hand and struck me. He walked out the door, slamming it behind him. Leaning back in my chair, I started to shake. While I was proud of myself for standing up to him, I remembered where that had led in the past.

That night, I had a prophetic dream about a conversation with my neighbor in the front house. She asked me not to let him come in through the yard anymore—she was

• Beyond Surviving

55

afraid for me. Just over two weeks later, there was a knock at my front door, and she was standing there. The conversation we had was the same one we had in my dream. This shook me to the core. I spent the rest of the day trying to remember what had happened at the end of my dream. I knew it was something bad, but it just wouldn't come to me.

On the following Friday as I was preparing to leave work, I got a phone call from Ward's preschool. There was a man who was trying to pick him up claiming to be his father. What did I want them to do? I dropped everything and ran to my car.

When I enrolled my son in the school, I left strict instructions not to release him to anyone but me. Thankfully, they followed my wishes but told me the man was sitting in his car across the street from the school and was very angry. I got there as soon as I could, and it was, indeed, Michael. I went to his car to talk to him. He was agitated and not making a lot of sense. I convinced him I would pick up Ward and his friend, who was staying the weekend, and go home. Then we could talk more.

I went into the school office and thanked the principal for following my instructions, calmed her down, and assured her that I would handle this. Mike wanted Ward to ride with him, but I said both boys were going to ride with me. He was upset that Ward had a friend coming over, but I told him it had already been agreed to with TJ's mom, and I wasn't going to change it at the last minute. The boys were really looking forward to it.

how "they were disappearing," hadn't I noticed? I wanted the boys to go play in the back, but he insisted they stay inside; that it wasn't safe, saying "they" had trucks going around picking people up off the streets. This continued through most of the night, and instead of being alarmed and concerned about the boys and my safety, I was focused in calming him down.

It's scary how easily I fell back onto that old pattern. He said he wanted to take Ward and me to the mountains where we could hide and be safe. He told me he had all his guns in the trunk of his car so he could protect us. I said no, that he was imagining things. He wanted to bring at least one gun into the house to protect us when they came for us. Again, I said no.

He called his mom and talked to her for a while and it seemed, without using the exact words, that he was saying goodbye to her. He also called Susi and again, seemed to be saying goodbye again. But it didn't set any alarms off because I was so worried about him. I should never have dropped my guard, and apparently my intuition regarding him seemed to be turned off. We hardly slept at all that night, so maybe I was just too tired to notice how bad things were.

Sunday morning, I was fixing a picnic so I could take the boys to the park for a while before TJ's mom came to pick him up. Mike was in the bedroom and called for me to come in with him. I finished making our lunch and packed it so that it was ready to go, then went into the bedroom. The boys were watching cartoons in the living room, laughing, and talking.

God and God's love earlier, and he wanted me to tell him more. I lay down facing him so I could talk to him. "No, no," he said, "I need you to turn over." Still no alarms!

I was reminding him that God was all-loving, and we just needed to turn things over to Him, that He would protect us. While I was talking, he was stroking the side of my face and tilting my head back a little. I started to turn back to him, but he stopped me and said, "No, I need you this way," so I continued. He kept stroking my face, saying, "I think I've got it," and he put his leg over the top of mine. It was getting really hard to talk with my head tilted back, and I started to turn again when I saw the knife out of my peripheral vision. But it was too late.

Now the alarms were clanging! He slashed my throat as I was trying to pull away. The sound of the knife ripping my flesh was in my head, like the sound of cutting raw meat. He must have momentarily loosened his hold on me because I rolled off the bed. He pounced on me and had me pinned beneath him. As he was holding the knife to my chest, and I was holding the blade, still talking and asking him why he was doing this.

Ward, who later told me he heard a strange sound, came into the room and saw what was happening. He jumped on Mike's back and started yelling at his dad and pounding his back with his small fists screaming at him to stop. "You're hurting my mom, look at all the blood!" he screamed. Mike was swinging his arm at Ward, telling him, "Get out of here! Get off me!" But Ward prevailed, and slowly, as if

I was afraid to look in the mirror but knew I had to get out of there or I would die. I tried to get Ward and TJ to come with me, but they were frozen in horror as the blood poured out of my throat and down my body. I stumbled out, leaving the boys there, knowing I would die if I stayed any longer and praying the boys wouldn't be hurt as I went into the alley.

I thought I saw someone and held out my hand asking for help, all the time praying for God to forgive Mike, that he was confused and didn't mean it. The man disappeared behind a hedge. I turned into the back of an apartment complex, thinking it's where I saw the man go. I didn't see anyone but could hear a TV. Going to the door, I knocked. No one came to answer, even though I thought I was pounding. Stumbling back down the steps to continue my search for help, I passed out. While unconscious, the entire attack replayed through my mind.

As my consciousness returned, I could feel the sun on my body and thought for a moment that I had washed my hair and was lying in the backyard drying it. Then the memory of the assault flooded back into my mind, and I tried to get up, but I was too weak from the loss of blood. Then I began to "bargain" with God. "Okay, I realize you're in charge here, but who will take care of Ward if I die? You'll have to find someone to raise him." At that point, I lost consciousness again.

When I woke up the second time, there was a man kneeling over me pushing something against my throat and telling bleeding, and that he had called 911, and the ambulance and the police were on their way. I told him I couldn't breathe, and he loosened the pressure enough for me to get a little air in. Then the police arrived. I gave them my address and told them Mike had guns, but I thought that they were in the trunk of his car in the garage, and my son and his little friend were in the house.

The ambulance arrived and they lifted me in. The doctor climbed in beside me, and we were rushed to Huntington Memorial Hospital and into the ER.

They were asking questions like "What happened?" and "Do you have insurance?" and were cutting my clothes off at the same time. I begged them not to cut my new bra, but they ignored me and continued what they were doing. I do remember the doctor who found me saying that it didn't matter whether or not I had insurance, that Huntington was a wealthy hospital, and the foundation would cover my costs and that I was to get a private room. It turned out that he was the head of emergency and that he and his wife had plans to go out. At the last moment they decided to stay home, so he was there when I needed him. Coincidence? I don't believe in those.

I don't remember them giving me blood, but I was told later that they gave me eight pints before they took me to surgery. I knew I was going to be okay as soon as the ER doctors began working on me. I was in and out of consciousness, and most of it was a blur, but I remember as they were pushing me to surgery that I asked what happened to my husband. When they didn't answer, I knew that he was dead.

"Switch your mentality from "I'm broken and helpless" to "I'm growing and healing" and watch how your life changes, for the better."

-Amazingmemovement.com

Chapter Six

A Time to Heal

I woke up hours later with bandages and a tracheotomy in a room with lots of machines around me and Mom and Dad sitting beside me. They both looked pretty grim, but their faces lit up momentarily when I opened my eyes. I drifted in and out of consciousness for the better part of a day. Mom told me that she spent the entire night watching the monitor just to reassure herself that I was breathing and my heart was still beating.

They were giving me morphine for the pain but had to discontinue it because it made me sick—not the greatest thing to happen when you have a throat wound. They really sorry when they took it away but understood that it was highly addictive. They asked me if I wanted it for pain or to sleep. I wasn't really in pain anymore, so they switched me to some kind of sleeping pill. It wasn't really as fast as the Demerol, but I guess it was better for my body. I was growing to depend on the drug after more than a week of regular injections.

I asked my parents how they got there—who notified them? They said Ward had given the police my address book and showed them the phone number to call. I asked where Ward was, and they told me the doctor and his wife agreed to keep him until they could pick him up. Over the course of the day, I was told they got the phone call, threw a few things together, jumped in the car, and drove as fast as possible. They stopped in Barstow to get my brothers, and not realizing that Michael was dead, they both grabbed their guns, and got to LA in record time.

The police who called them said when police arrived at my place and announced their presence, two little boys opened the front door and came out with their hands raised saying "Don't shoot, we're the good guys." Ward later told me they heard the noises in the bathroom and guessed what was happening. Michael had locked himself in my bathroom and slashed his own throat with the same knife he'd used on me, then stabbed himself a number of times in the chest. He was already dead by the time the police arrived. The whole bathroom was a bloody mess. I'm glad he had the presence of mind to lock the door. I can't imagine how

The doctor's wife came over and said she would watch the boys until someone came to get them. TJ's mom was called, she came to pick him up, and Ward was alone with strangers in the midst of this whole crazy mess.

Mom and dad first went to Ward and told him he had been very brave and that they were going to the hospital to see me. He wanted to see me too, but they didn't know what shape I was in and wanted to be sure I was going to make it before allowing him to go, so they told him he was too young to visit. He was furious, so I was told, and kept stomping around saying he was really mad. I was glad to hear that he was speaking his feelings, but the doctor's wife, with the best of intentions, kept trying to shush and calm him down, telling him everything would be all right. I'm afraid that had lasting consequences regarding his ability or inability to talk about his feelings because he started acting out instead.

The hospital made an exception to their "too young to visit" rule and let my poor, frightened little boy in to see me. Unfortunately, they hadn't bothered washing the blood out of my hair, and he carried that image with him the rest of his life. But at least he saw that I was alive.

Once I was on the post-surgical floor, they let TJ come see that I was going to be okay. Both boys needed the visual reassurance. It was a very traumatic experience for anyone, let alone someone so young. Ward had just turned six years old in February of that year, and TJ was around the same age.

moved onto a regular floor. I still had a private room, but they moved a bed in for my mom. And that's when I really found out how many people really cared for me. I had almost non-stop visitors. The nurses came to check on me and clean my tracheostomy two or three times a day. They put a suction tube down my throat through the tube inserted for breathing and "cleaned my throat." Imagine have a vacuum "cleaning" your lungs. It was not a pleasant experience.

Sometime later, the social worker from the hospital came to see me. She and I "talked "about hospital business. I say "talked" because I had to write everything down at that point; I couldn't literally talk because my vocal cords had been severed and needed time to heal. She told me California had a fund to pay the medical expenses of victims of violent crimes and that she applied on my behalf. That was a huge relief, as I had no idea how I was going to pay for all this. I had only recently started a new job and didn't have health insurance yet.

I told her that I needed to do something—I needed to pay this experience forward to other women who were feeling trapped in a similar situation so they wouldn't come to a similar ending. She thought this was a wonderful idea. Before I was released, the director of The Haven came to see me, and she said she would see what she could do to facilitate an opportunity.

At one point, my doctor insisted I limit my visitors, but I told him no, that they were helping me more than the quiet time I had to just think. He finally agreed but told mom to monitor my rest.

on both sides, and the esophagus. The doctor wished the knife had been sharper because there was significant tearing of the flesh but somehow managed to miss any nerves. That, he said was a miracle. The doctor mentioned all this to me almost as an afterthought, which totally freaked me out. Can you imagine being told you might never speak again? It scared me into total compliance with the doctor's instructions and infused me with a fierce determination to heal quickly.

I wished Ruth, my original therapist, could come. I had a great rapport with her, but she and her family moved out of state. Before she left, she referred me to a man. She felt I would progress further by talking with a compassionate male. So, my new therapist came to see me, but he was so nervous he made me uncomfortable. When he discovered I couldn't speak and had to write everything down, he insisted on writing back to me instead of just speaking. I don't know if he felt that would put him on my level or if he was uncomfortable speaking when I could not, but the result was that I asked him not to come back.

Susi came almost every day, and I spent as much or more time comforting her as she did me. Women from the shelter and the support group took turns stopping in to see how I was doing. That's when I remembered that my husband had been rated a" ten," meaning he was judged the most dangerous of abusers. One of them told me when they got the call from the police, they were immediately sure it was me. Other friends from work came to see me too. I'll never forget how Anna couldn't look at me at first. When I asked

While I was there, another woman was brought in who had been attacked by a burglar. Her throat had also been slashed. My nurses thought it might be a good idea, if I was up to it, for me to go "talk" to her. I was okay with that, but the other woman didn't want to see anyone. What is it about men who try to silence women this way?

My ex-sister-in-law and her brother came to visit. He mentioned that Deb told him not to get his hopes up. Because I had lost so much blood, I may be little more than a vegetable. I was more than happy to prove her wrong.

I wanted to go and see Michael's body before he was cremated. I instructed mom that he needed to be in a casket so his family could see him, and I needed to see his body to make his death real to me. I asked my doctor if I could go. At first, he said no—no way could I leave the hospital—but I kept pleading my case because I needed to know he was, in fact, really dead. Dad had told me that he was, but the whole incident had taken on a dreamlike quality, and I had to be sure.

Finally, after speaking with the hospital board, my doctor said I could go if I could get a nurse to go with me and if I used an ambulance. Every one of my nurses volunteered to accompany me, but the hospital said they could not because of the liability it would create. Then another miracle—my best friend from college, Pat, walked into my room and said she would be happy to ride along with me (and had the requisite RN behind her name). We had been estranged for several years due to the total isolation I'd control over the victim.

I was so grateful to Pat for coming back into my life at that point in time. We picked up right where we had left off in our friendship. So, it was decided, I could go and put my mind at ease. The trip from Pasadena to the mortuary in Inglewood was surreal. Pat and I barely said a word. I was lost in my own thoughts, and I suppose she was too.

As we turned into the mortuary, one I had been to numerous times for family funerals, I was overcome with feelings. The director escorted me into the viewing room and left me alone with the casket and my feelings. Pat hovered in the background as I looked down at the body of the man I had spent the last twenty years of my life with. If they hadn't assured me it was Michael, I would not have been able to recognize him. They had dressed him in a turtleneck to cover his throat and the stab marks in his chest. He had on a lot of makeup, and his sneer was missing.

I was overcome with emotion, and Pat had come in to stand by me. It seemed like such a waste. Even though he had tried to kill me, I felt sorrow for him. How scared he must have been in his last moments. I touched his dead body and hoped he had found the peace he was looking for. As hard as it had been to look at him, lying there, I knew it had been necessary for me. Even so, he haunted me for months. I had dreams. The worst one was when I was at home and looked out the window to see him standing across the street, laughing at me, telling me it had all been an elaborate hoax, and he was still going to get me. I woke up filled with terror but could remind myself that I'd seen

I was gaining more strength every day. Sometimes when my nurse came to get me for a walk around the floor, we would skip just to make her laugh. The nurses I had were the best, and they made my stay a good experience. One of them stayed in touch, and we did things together for a while after I was back home. We went to the Pantages Theater to see "A Chorus Line," which I still love to this day. We also went up into the mountains outside of Frazier Park and went horseback riding. It was fabulous to be out in the beautiful country, feeling the sun on my face and the breeze blowing my hair.

During my hospital stay, I also learned that people are willing to go the extra mile to help and support you when you're in need. I was only in the hospital for a total of thirteen days, a stay much briefer than they anticipated. I believe the outpouring of love and support had a lot to do with my rapid healing.

The night before I was released, Mom and Dad brought wine and dinner. I had only started eating solid foods the day before. Steak was too hard for me to swallow, and the wine burned my throat. I tried to eat it anyway because it meant so much to them. It seems, in retrospect, that I had spent a lot of my life taking care of others instead of taking care of myself.

After I left the hospital, Ward and I returned to our house in the Van Nuys. While I had been hospitalized my parents came down to help me. Dad cleaned up our little rental house in South Pasadena and they made Michael's funeral

I felt he was traumatized enough. It may have been a mistake on my part, but I was trying to protect my son.

The director of The Haven called to let me know that the TV program *Two on the Town* was interested in interviewing me when I was able to talk again. My new life was beginning all over again.

*"No matter what Life may throw your
way, never underestimate your ability
to conquer defeat of any kind."*

-Heather D. Wright

Chapter Seven

Rebuilding a Life

I learned that Michael had filed the quitclaim deed he forced me to sign and had taken out a private second mortgage, interest only, on the house. That meant that two weeks after I got out of the hospital, the balloon payment of $24,000 was due. That was added to the pile of things I had to wade through once I got home.

Mom and Dad stayed with me for the first several weeks. Mom took me to doctor appointments, and when I was home, I had to go through all of Michael's things and distribute them. My brothers were happy to take most of the tools, records, and even clothes that Mike left behind. The find the money to pay her off. We owned several pieces of property. I sold one to pay off the loan, and Dad refurbished the front house on the property Mike's mom lived on so I could rent it out and have some income while I recovered.

It was hard going through everything that reminded me of the twenty years we had been together. I found a little spiral notebook Michael had been keeping and went through it hoping to find some clue to his behavior that final weekend. One entry may have been what I was looking for. It read, "Soul Swapping…as we pass on," and I wondered if that's what he was trying to do. Why he would want to swap souls with me I couldn't begin to understand, but it was something to think about. I knew he was reading a lot of metaphysical books, but it was beyond me at the time. He also noted from the Lord's prayer, "on Earth as it is in Heaven?", but again, it was a mystery as to why he noted this phrase.

I began to read a lot of poetry about loss and allowed myself to go through the stages of denial, anger, bargaining, grief, and acceptance .In the grief stage, I wrote a poem to my late husband, "As my words splash across the page, like falling tears, I cry, what a loss." I wrote it on a napkin while sitting in my bed crying. Those were hard weeks, trying to pick up my life and get through all the sadness and fear that followed me. I woke up one morning, drenched in sweat from a bad dream about Michael swearing he would still find a way to get me.

Ward, in the meantime, was happy to be home and pick up the friendships he had been forced to leave behind. I other things on my mind. So, I just told him that I had not, and that Michael had, in fact, killed himself.

Dad eventually went home, but Mom stayed another several weeks. She was terrified I would choke and die if I was alone. She was such a comfort to have around, and I could never thank her enough for helping me through the hardest time of my life. But all things come to an end. She went home because she and Dad had rented a houseboat on Lake Powell for the family to vacation on together. Both Mom and Dad begged me to come along, but I still had an open trach in my throat, and the doctor said I would drown if I fell in the water. The thought of it really scared me. So, I sent Ward, but stayed home myself. It was a chance for him to do something fun with his cousins and take his mind off recent occurrences in his short life.

I got Ward enrolled in a kindergarten a few blocks from the house and took my time alone to volunteer at the Southern California Coalition on Battered Women. There I found purpose and a community of like-minded women—women who were tired of other women being punching bags, physical and/or verbal, for men who were upset or disappointed about their lives.

There was a walk scheduled to happen where the walkers would get sponsors to pay for every mile they walked. I helped mail out the invitations and signed my neighborhood up to sponsor me. It was five miles long and there was to be a rally in a neighborhood park in Santa Monica, where I would be a featured speaker.

on a mission. I completed the walk, and there were celebrity speakers on before me. I had been assigned a woman, Patti Giggins, to be my bodyguard in case there were any "crazies" in the crowd. When it was my turn to take the stage, the microphone mysteriously failed, so one of the celebrities picked up a bullhorn and stepped up beside me. My entire speech I whispered to her, and she relayed it to the crowd.

I whispered because my voice, at that time, sounded like Minnie Mouse, and I thought whispering would be more effective. You know that old adage "if you want to get someone's attention, whisper"? It was very empowering, and the crowd responded enthusiastically. The fundraiser was a huge success. The following day I received a gorgeous floral arrangement from my celebrity, and the card read "You're my hero." That same celebrity later exposed that she had been a battered woman and wrote a book about her experience.

It was also the first time in my life I had been introduced to so many strong women, some of whom were also lesbians. I had a stereotypical image of who and what a lesbian was, and these women didn't fit that image. They were just like any other woman who had a good sense of who they were and wanted to use that strength to help other women find their own inner strength. I was accepted into this amazing group of women and felt like I had come home. We had a common goal, and all worked towards it in our own way, but also as a community.

"women's music" at the VA in West L.A. It was Chris Williamson's Blue Rider concert, and her music was so moving I had tears running down my face half the time she was on stage performing. That music helped change my view of the world we live in, and I wrote, but never sent, my first and only fan letter.

I spent my days working at the Southern California Coalition on Battered Women and learned a lot of helpful information. Then I got a call from the *Two on the Town* producers. They wanted to interview me. We set up an appointment for them to come to my house to do the interview.

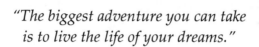

*"The biggest adventure you can take
is to live the life of your dreams."*

-Oprah Winfrey

Chapter Eight

A New Life

The day of the interview with *Two on the Town* arrived, I was so nervous yet so wonderfully excited. This would be the new start of my new life. I had been blessed with a second chance! I was determined to make my new life's focus be on helping others. I didn't want anyone suffering the nightmare like the one I had lived through.

I had a morning appointment in Long Beach with some women who worked in a shelter for battered women. They were planning a march to raise awareness of the amount of spousal abuse happening every day, and they asked me if I would participate and speak at the after-rally. We brainstormed what needed to be done to make this march

At lunchtime, I had just half an hour to rush back to my house in Van Nuys for the interview with the *Two on the Town* hosts. It was a long drive back. I had to fight the legendary L.A. traffic, but I made it. The television crew arrived just as I was pulling into my driveway. The timing was perfect.

They wanted the details of the attack and talked to me about my future, how I would cope with life after abuse, and battered women in general. They took a video of me standing at the kitchen counter cutting up a melon, perhaps just to show me as a regular woman doing a normal household task of preparing food. They were there for about an hour total, then left to return to the studio and edit the piece. I felt it went okay, and they sent me a tape of the show after it aired. Several months later they sent me a notice that the episode had won a Peabody Award. As far as I know, it was the only prestigious award they received for that show, and they were thrilled! I was overjoyed that it had made enough of an impact to win the Peabody!

It got to the point that I was approached practically every time I left the house by people who wanted to let me know they had seen the show and were deeply affected. Most of them knew of someone who had experienced domestic violence but had no idea it was so widespread. Being approached like that made me feel somewhat awkward. I didn't know how to handle it, except to thank them and hope they had a better understanding of the issue. It seemed that while I was trying to get the message out into

I was really anxious to get more involved. There were several possibilities being tossed around to broaden my audience, but I had to get back to work and make a living for Ward and me. As if on cue, my boss from United Geophysical called. He needed someone to replace the accountant on the main set of books at Forest Lawn in Glendale. He asked if I would be interested, and we met for lunch.

He remembered my excellent work from United Geophysical and hoped I was well enough to take the position he was offering me. The problem, it seemed, was that they were in the process of converting their accounting records from a manual system to an electronic system using computers; the current accountant couldn't get it done. So, the following Monday I reported for work. I had worked with some of the other people before in Pasadena, so it wasn't like walking in cold to a new environment. The former accountant was transferred to a different position. It was a happy solution for everyone. The old accountant was in a position he could handle; I had a job, and IT had an accounting partner with whom they felt confidant.

Forest Lawn was the largest privately held corporation in the U.S. at that time. The cemeteries themselves are beautiful, and I would often sit outside during my lunch break beside a lily pond with statuary and a fountain from Europe with lush green lawns spreading away from the edge. It was very much like working amid an indoor/outdoor work of art.

followed by singing patriotic and family picnic-type songs. The agenda was set by the owners and no dissention was tolerated. I drew the line at them telling me how I was expected to vote and stopped going. When questioned about my absence, I told them I had work to finish for the month-end closing of the books. I guess that was an acceptable excuse because it related to the company money. I never had to subject myself to those meetings again.

The dress code was as antiquated as the meetings, something else irksome to me and others. I took it upon myself to change it. By the time I left the company, women were allowed to wear pantsuits instead of dresses, and men could wear slacks instead of a suit.

Getting back to work, my life slowly began to feel like normality was returning. I was starting to go out socially with friends, dining and dancing, and generally starting to feel alive again. I was also beginning to have sexual feelings again—reaffirming life. It's a common reaction after death has come very close to you, I later found out. I guess I had been experiencing PTSD pretty strongly but as I dived back into life it began to affect me less and less. The daily routine normalized my feelings and thoughts of the attack were getting to be fewer and farther away.

One evening after drinks and dancing, I agreed to go with the man I'd been dancing with to continue our evening. He asked me to follow him and led me to a motel. While he was inside getting a room, I realized what was happening and panicked. I slammed the car into reverse and sped away. I could see in the rearview mirror that he up to me. I was terrified and drove even faster, but he kept up.

I exited the freeway in a part of town I wasn't familiar with and was driving down streets and turning corners trying to lose him, but he was yelling at me to pull over. I finally turned a corner and found myself on a dead-end street. He pulled up behind me, boxing me in, and demanded I roll down the window and talk to him—he just wanted to talk. He said if I had changed my mind all I had to do was tell him. As we talked, I calmed down and realized he meant me no harm and ended up having him follow me home. We stayed up talking some more, and eventually he leaned in to kiss me. We did end up in bed, and it was definitely life-affirming, but it left me feeling totally unfulfilled. I didn't go back to that place again. I didn't want him to be there and recognize me.

Several months later, I was out to dinner with girlfriends. We stayed awhile after our meal to watch the dancing and listen to the music while we continued catching up. There were some men at a table near ours who were talking, and one of them asked me if I was a popular singer with a breathy, raspy voice. I laughed and told them no, but thanks for the compliment. He came over and asked if I'd like to dance. We talked for quite a while and spent a very pleasant evening together. It was fun and totally nonthreatening. He asked if he could take me to lunch the next week.

When the day arrived, he picked me up and we went to a nearby restaurant with an outdoor patio for Mexican-style dining. There were Jacaranda trees in full bloom shading excited, but he was really nice and easy to talk with. We had a pitcher of sangria with our lunch and spent a pleasant couple of hours getting to know one another. By the time he took me back to work, I was floating in a pleasant bubble as we made arrangements to meet again.

The only problem was, he was married. I didn't want to be an issue in the marriage, but he was so nice and so much fun I decided we could be friends with occasional benefits. One day he brought me a couple of concert catalogs and told me to pick out some that I would like to go see. I saw Bette Midler at The Greek Theater and James Taylor and Joan Baez at Universal Studios. We spent a week in Laguna Beach together and had a wonderful time. He had some work with him, so I roamed the little beach town, read a book, swam in the ocean, and took long walks along the beach.

He called his wife several times while we were there together. I felt guilty, so we talked about it and agreed that we would remain friends only from that point forward. Dan and I are still friends, and I'm friends with his second wife as well. His first wife and I also became friends.

I was still going to the support group I'd joined after I left the shelter. My fellow group members, along with the moderator, were encouraging me to see a counselor. I was reluctant. I couldn't see why going deeper and deeper into my failed, abusive relationship was going to set me free and help me feel better about moving forward.

My friend who I used to ride horses with, had come back into my life while I was in the hospital. She had been and she found a handsome yearling, a rose grey stallion. His sire was the grand National Champion, Kharibe, and he was beauty in motion. Even his name appealed to me—Kharibe' s Sprite. She made an appointment, and we drove out to the ranch to take a look.

I fell in love with him immediately. He was beautiful, fluid in gait, and full of fire. He also made me laugh with his antics. His owner and I discussed price, and I was really happy that he could possibly be mine. Nevertheless, it was out of my budget, and with a heavy heart I had to pass. Six months later, she called me and said she had gelded him for trying to jump fences to get to the mares which dropped his price, and would I be interested in reconsidering? I was ecstatic! A week later, he was mine. One of the better decisions I ever made.

I moved him to the ranch where my friend kept her horse and began learning, as I went along, what went into gentling a horse for riding. One of my nurses from the hospital loaned me her tack box so I didn't have to buy everything new, and I began. This was my way of getting therapy. Have you ever had a two-ton animal at the other end of a rope that hadn't been worked before? It took my full concentration, partly because it was all new to me and partly because he was learning and not always in agreement with what I was trying to teach him.

I made the mistake of allowing myself to be distracted, just for a few seconds, and he bolted away from me, pulling the rope through my ungloved hands. It burned the skin so bad that I dropped the rope and ran to the owner's house his stall. I never worked him again without gloves. Some lessons one learns the hard way.

I continued working with him, and he gradually went from working on a lunge line to accepting a bridle. Next came the saddle, which made him a bit nervous, but by then he trusted me and accepted it. By the time I was ready to get on him, I slid down from the top of the fence onto his back, and his only reaction was to turn his head and look at me, like saying "What are you doing up there?"

I'd get home from work, change clothes, and head for the ranch. Ward loved it too because it meant usually stopping at McDonalds for food first. The ranch owner had a couple of kids for him to play with when he didn't want to watch me work with Sprite.

Meanwhile, I continued to work within the battered women's community as often as possible, and they were working to find a more permanent place for me. I met with a reporter for the Los Angeles Herald Examiner for an interview. We met together several times to address follow-up questions she had. She finished the article, and it was published. It was featured in the Style section on the front page and ran for two consecutive days. A friend, the head of the Southern California Coalition on Battered Women, called me the day it came out and thanked me. She said her parents read it, and for the first time, they truly understood why she was doing the work she chose.

It was a great feeling to know I helped someone who had opened doors into the Battered Women's community for

After the newspaper closed, she relocated to the east coast to teach. She returned to L.A. a couple of times, and we always spent some time together.

About six months after the article in the Examiner ran, I was offered the position of Community Educator at Sojourn, a battered women's shelter. Overjoyed, I was really getting started doing what mattered so much to me. My job was to reach out into the community for groups to teach about the issue and severity of domestic violence in their world and that domestic violence crossed all socioeconomic boundaries. At that time, most people thought only the poor or women of color experienced abuse at home.

I also started and moderated support groups wherever requested. I shared my story with them as a way to connect despite our differences. I even started a group for battered lesbians—apparently, it never occurred to anyone else.

It was also my job to make any media appearances on behalf of Sojourn. That *Two on the Town* interview I did was the first of many televised interviews over the next six years. My partner told me kiddingly that she couldn't take me anywhere without being recognized. It was overwhelming for a while.

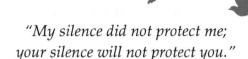

"My silence did not protect me;
your silence will not protect you."

-Audre Lorde

Chapter Nine

Breaking My Silence

Finally, my first day arrived and pretty much evolved the same way most first days in a new position do; signing paperwork, meeting with the director to be filled in on what she expected from me, and signing up for volunteer training so I would be able to answer hotline calls using the correct protocol.

As it turned out, I had to pretty much create my space. The staff were welcoming and supportive, and I jumped right in. There were copies of handouts the woman before me put together, and I created a training manual to use when speaking to any group. This would be the first time they had a dedicated position for community education, that I built my platform to bring awareness to the public about the frequency of this insidious crime and what victims had to deal with. I also added the information a victim could use to help themselves when they decided to leave their abuser.

There were weekend get-togethers where we brought food, cooked it together, and listened to music—an informal bonding of women with a common goal. Through these women, I found a comfortable place and felt like a whole new world had opened for me.

Audiences were growing and becoming more frequent. But the two most frequent questions I got were still "What about men? Aren't they abused too?" and "Why doesn't she just leave?"

Men are abused too, but much less frequently than women, but men are also less likely to report abuse. Their abuse usually comes in the form of ridicule rather than violent physical abuse, although that can happen as well. This is not to minimize the damage verbal and emotional abuse inflicts. That kind of abuse is emotionally crippling. It strips away self-confidence and leaves self-doubt in its place. One of my handouts is a copy of an article written by Audre Lorde titled "The Bruise That Doesn't Heal" that speaks directly to verbal abuse. However, men constitute 2 percent to 4 percent of domestic abuse victims, while women make up 96 percent to 98 percent of the victims. That is why I focused on the female victims.

able to take care of themselves and/or their children. Many women come from families where there was abuse, so they think abuse is normal and don't see why leaving would make any difference, or why their next relationship wouldn't just be more of the same.

When you are in this situation, your life quickly becomes survival, not living, and it's hard to realize that you are strong. The proof of your strength is in what you live through—sometimes daily. But when you're in the midst of it, you don't have the time alone to think and get any clarity. And you certainly aren't thinking *I'm choosing to stay; I can choose to leave.* That concept is not one that most in an abusive situation can conceive in their present. I certainly couldn't. But after years of learning and healing, I can now recognize that truth.

I went to the West Coast Women's Music and Comedy Festival with a friend. It was a destination on Labor Day weekend I kept for as long as it was available. The first time was in Santa Barbara County. There were craftswomen, workshops, and speeches during the day. We swam in the river just below the Reagan Ranch and laughed at our audacity. It was for women only, and we were in various stages of undress for a long weekend. Women built the stages, did the wiring for electricity and sound, cooked, and barbequed. It was a sensual banquet that we soaked up—colors, music and education all displayed by, and presented by women.

I'd never had such an experience in my life and it affected me profoundly. I was introduced to so many new things wearing a shirt.

In the ensuing years, I started volunteering at the festival. The volunteers arrived on "the land" a week before the "festies" and set the entire venue up, from building two stages, organizing the kitchen, setting out bleach by the port-a-potties, clearing weeds from the concert areas, to doing inventory of souvenirs. We had a pool on this site. It was right outside the western portal to Yosemite and so beautiful. Wandering the land "sky clad," we tanned all over, felt the gentle breeze against our skin to keep us from overheating from the sun, and felt free.

By the time the last festival came, I had a life- partner, and we oversaw the night concession at the main stage. It was magical and spiritual at the same time. It was a time in my life I'll always remember with love and appreciation. It created a profound opening of my eyes and showed me how cooperation worked better than following someone's orders simply by involving everyone in the process.

One day, I had a vision in one of the daytime spiritual circles. We had been meditating and chanting. I closed my eyes and felt myself drift up into the sky where I was joined by three other women representing other races, and I was white. We joined hands and encircled the globe, protecting mother earth together. It was powerful and reinforced my belief that we're all connected, and that women are the spiritual protectors.

One night during the music we were treated to a meteor shower that seemed to be just at the top of the hill behind us.

took center stage, and it went on for quite a few minutes.

I began by building a network with the other shelters in the Southern California area and reaching out to civic organizations. I was invited to join the Domestic Violence Council of Los Angeles, which broadened my outreach. Whenever a call came into Sojourn asking for a speaker, it was referred to me.

Soon I was appearing on local and national television programs as well as radio shows, being interviewed to spread the awareness of the issues of domestic violence. But they always wanted me to recall my final episode with my husband when he slashed my throat. I did everything I could to minimize my experience and promote the idea of how widespread this issue truly was/is.

At first, it was pretty heavy stuff that they all wanted to talk to me about, but I quickly realized it was the sensation they were after, and the message was secondary as far as they were concerned. It was frustrating because I wanted the focus to be on the issue of widespread domestic violence, not just my story. My motivation was to bring awareness and education to the audiences, not just to titillate them.

One of the groups I was assigned to represent Sojourn in was a Community Health Fair. It was the most significant assignment of my life. I was busy handing out stickers and fact sheets and answering questions as to why I was at a health fair when one of the nurses taking blood pressures caught my eye. I saw her wandering around looking at the different booths. She was taller than me by a few inches,

I was so nervous and afraid I would stutter. She asked me a couple of questions about why I was there, why did a battered women's shelter belong at a health fair?

Later, I walked by her booth, looked straight up into her eyes and boldly said, "You are the most attractive woman I've ever seen." It certainly caught both of us off guard and she blushed. When she offered to take my blood pressure, I passed, telling her I would probably blow up her machine. —Then I casually walked back to my space.

She stopped by later and said she was taking a break and asked if I would like to join her. And that was the beginning of our lifelong relationship. She grounds me, and after thirty-nine years, my heart still belongs to Lynn. As far as I'm concerned, she is my gift from the Universe, and I'm glad I was open to accept her.

"I always wondered why someone didn't do something about that. Then I realized I was somebody."

-Lily Tomlin

Chapter Ten

Advocacy

Advocacy is to change "what is" into "what should be."

I joined the California Coalition Against Domestic Violence (CCADV) at their invitation. CAADV is a state-wide coalition representing the varied parts of the state. Southern California, Northern California, Central California, and vast rural areas in the north were all represented, so all types of constituents would have their specific issues addressed. Urban versus rural and northern versus southern all have specific needs that had to be addressed.

We were working with California Senator Robert Presley to promote the passage of his bill that required police in 1986. Domestic violence was, and still is, the most dangerous call a police officer can respond to. According to a study done in 2019 by the US Department of Justice, 40 percent of officers killed in the line of duty happen when officers respond to Domestic Violence calls.

Practically every day people hear on the news about a woman being killed by a husband, boyfriend, or ex-husband/boyfriend. It's the most prevalent violent crime and should be placed at the top of the list of crimes to eradicate. Think about how domestic terrorism has come to the forefront in the past year, so why not do the same for domestic violence?

We at the CAADV worked hard to get this bill passed, going to the state capital and speaking to various senators. We were told we were the most successful non-profit lobbying organization in the state, even though we were the smallest. When the bill became law, several of us from the CCADV were asked to join police, sheriffs, and district attorneys on a task force convened by the California Attorney General to write the curriculum for the required training. It was a change in the way things were being done—including the women in the CAADV as experts in the issue and not solely law enforcement.

In the meantime, Mom and Dad would come down to stay with Ward so he could continue school and have someone to come home to afterwards. I couldn't have taken him with me.

right for the curriculum. It was a task I found both interesting and frustrating. We, the advocates, wanted to ensure that the content dealt with the issues. The law-and-order members of the commission were more concerned about the use of correct action words— should, could, can, will, etc.—which was frustrating. Some days I felt like screaming or tearing my hair out!

It wasn't all work, because when we finished the day's work, we went out for dinner. Every evening we gathered, had a nice meal, and chatted as friends. Some of the police were from LA, and I worked with them on the Domestic Violence Council. We relaxed and shared stories while talking about our current project.

Friday afternoons, they would all fly home, and my fun weekend began. After Lynn left work on Friday, she would join me, sometimes driving, sometimes flying to the city I was in. We enjoyed exploring the surrounding area of each city.

We went through the California Mission in Monterey, founded by Fr. Junipero Serra, and drove into Carmel. We wandered around and looked in the inviting storefronts of various shops. We had lunch at a little bistro, sitting outside in the patio and did a little people watching. I kept their tiny expresso spoons as a souvenir. Then, we drove down Highway 1 to Big Sur and enjoyed a Mexican Coffee at Nepenthe, a restaurant perched high at the top of the cliffs overlooking the Pacific Ocean and made famous in the film "The Sandpipers," starring Elizabeth Taylor.

a watercolor of an old barn under a full moon from an artist displaying her paintings. It's a nostalgic, somewhat dreamy piece, and it still graces our living room wall. On one of our walks, I found an ancient, rusted, railroad spike I still keep as a wonderful memento of our special time together. We even took in an opera matinee. Lynn loves it and Tosca, her favorite opera, was playing; it seemed too perfect an opportunity to pass up. We were definitely dressed too casually for the opera, as most of the women were wearing their finest dresses and furs. I kept whispering to Lynn, "Look at all the dead animals." She kept shushing me, trying to look very stern but giggling at the same time.

Sacramento has a great "old town" too, and we enjoyed every minute of it. We walked around the capital building and stuffed ourselves with seafood fresh from the river. I showed her the Attorney General's office where I was working on the curriculum to train law enforcement, allowing for our weekends. We paid for the days after the committee meetings concluded, but because I was part of the committee, I paid government rates.

In San Francisco we went to Fisherman's Wharf for the famous fresh seafood and had Irish coffee at the Buena Vista restaurant. We walked around listening to street performers and looking at the creations of local artists. Lynn bought me an ocarina shaped like a dolphin. It was a little out of tune but fun to play. I keep it on my nightstand now and every time I see it, I remember that weekend and the love it represents. When Lynn's daughter asked her why she spent

In Anaheim, we spent a day at Disneyland. It really invites your inner child out to play; a welcome break from the heartache and pain I had dealt with not so long ago on a daily basis.

In Fresno, we drove up into the foothills of the beautiful, magnificent, Sierra Nevada Mountains. We lost ourselves in the breathtaking splendor that was created to refresh our souls and was so special. I'm drawn to mountains, and we breathed the cool mountain air and discovered fool's gold. From the river's edge, it looked like sparkling flashes as the sunlight struck it in the clear water. Fools' gold looks just like real gold flakes, but it floats when disturbed. Real gold is heavy and sinks to the bottom. My dad's father was a miner, and I learned this little tidbit as a child of eight years when my family first visited Yosemite.

In San Jose we explored the Winchester House built by Sarah Winchester to ease the spirits of victims of her husband's creation. To say it rambled is an understatement. There are stairways that lead to locked doors with nothing on the other side, and one that leads to the ceiling. The stairs are so tiny you have to walk sideways for your feet to fit on the steps, and I have small feet. It was fascinating to see what someone with enough money would create to appease spirits no longer on this plane. She continued construction until her death because she believed that if she stopped, the spirits would become angry. We looked for the San Jose California Mission, but it's actually in Fremont.

the construction of words put together, the different factions came to better understand the trials each one grappled with daily. By understanding each other, we became a unit moving toward a common goal. Perhaps if every issue was broken down and rebuilt in this manner, we could move closer to focusing on our commonalities rather than our differences and come together for the greater good.

One of the lessons I learned by working in a women's community was how to reach a consensus—a solution that worked for all, not just a few. Interestingly enough, that is how our committee of law enforcement and victim advocates created the curriculum.

Once the curriculum was complete, our committee disbanded, and the real work began—training law enforcement officers about safer and more effective ways to respond to a domestic violence incident. I was invited to train LAPD, Torrance PD, Long Beach PD, and the Sheriffs in the Santa Clarita Valley. Initially, I anticipated resistance, and I got it, mostly from senior officers who resented a civilian "telling them how to do their job."

One of the examples I used of an ineffective call was my experience when the police were called to my house. "The police knocked on the front door and announced themselves. Michael told me to get in the bathroom and clean myself up. I could hear him laughing with the officers and saying that even if he had hit me, I deserved it, and they laughed too. It didn't give me a feeling of safety." That gave them something to think about.

to chat with them individually and without others hearing what we talked about. This "off" time was when some of them would open up and ask more personal questions. After the training class ended, I passed out evaluation forms and, for the most part, got good reviews. A few of the guys asked if I was available to do private trainings.

One said I had opened his eyes. He never thought about verbal and emotional abuse and that he had been being abusive to his wife without thinking, but he never laid a hand on her. He asked what he could do, and we had a productive conversation. He stayed in touch and later, even after his wife left him, he thanked me. He helped me understand that I was on the right path.

My initial contact inside LAPD was on the Domestic Violence Council and the AG's committee. He told me he had suggested that I should be paid a stipend of $50 per training session. It was approved, and though I never received it, I was happy that the work was being validated and it opened the door for the next person to continue the trainings.

As my presence for trainings became more in demand, I found my fellow workers back at Sojourn pulling away from me. The day came when the director spoke to me about how it wasn't fair to the other staff that I received so much attention when they, the others, were working just as hard or harder behind the scenes. She settled this by redefining my position and putting me in a part-time role.

After four years and several uncomfortable months, I submitted my letter of resignation. I felt I was being punished for being too successful at the task assigned to me in the first place but also felt it must mean it was time for me to move on. The Universe was nudging me.

"Opportunities don't happen, you create them."

-Chris Grosser

Chapter Eleven

Inside The System

Before I resigned from Sojourn, I was approached by two different agencies with job opportunities that were looking for my experience and knew me both personally and professionally. One was the Los Angeles Commission on Assaults Against Women, the other was a Department of Justice grant in the Los Angeles City Attorney's office. I wasn't sure which one would give me more experience, so I asked several friends from the L.A. Domestic Violence Council for their input. The decision I made was to go with the City Attorney's office since I had worked outside the legal system at this point and was told I would make a bigger contribution to victims by working inside the government.

with glass walls in the corners. My only exposure to a governmental agency up to that point was from TV where they each had their own office. Each ACA, Assistant City Attorney, was assigned a desk and a phone, and they were all quite busy.

I met with the attorney who had recruited me and also happened to be my supervisor. She went over my responsibilities, and we created a working plan. I went to get fingerprinted and bonded. Most of the first day was taken up with completing the necessary steps for my official hire. I was working under a Department of Justice grant and was being paid by the Mayor's Office, not the Office of the City Attorney. It was all very convoluted, and I was never paid the amount the DOJ assigned me—something about a feud between the Mayor's Office and the City Attorney's office.

Shortly after starting my new job, my supervisor and I were invited to attend a national meeting on domestic violence being held in Tulsa, OK. There were several women I had met before from other parts of the country in attendance. We introduced ourselves and developed an agenda that could be used nationally for the treatment and assistance of victims of domestic violence. When we adjourned, we were treated to a nice meal and an outdoor enactment of the play, "Oklahoma."

We left with great contacts and a sense of how we would be a part of a national network of women focused on stopping domestic violence. At the time, California was the only state with a victim advocate program inside the criminal

I went to work designing an advocacy program. It had been tried before but never really took off. It was met with a certain amount of resistance from the attorneys. The last attempt had failed to implement a program designed to offer assistance to the women who were trying to get help from a system which was stacked against them.

These women were initially told that if the abuser was going to be prosecuted, they were the ones that had to prosecute him. I explained the way it actually worked was it would really be the State of California versus the abuser. They did have to press charges, they had to tell the police when they arrived on a call that the abuser had, in fact, attacked them, but it was the State who was prosecuting the defendant—not the victim. The victim was a witness, not the prosecutor.

Too many times, forty years later, the abuser is still told to take a walk and cool off. Forming the task force was an uphill battle, but it helped because someone from my team would be with the woman through the entire process, including any court appearances needed. These women are terrified because they have talked to their husbands or boyfriends who are very apologetic, sometimes telling them that it will "never happen again." The women want to believe this because life wasn't always so bad. They have little-to-no self-esteem left and can't begin to believe they can make it on their own, especially if there are children involved.

want to be in jail. In fact, abusers are encouraged to do this by their attorney because most of the time it works, and the attorney's job load is lightened. My job was to convince the abused women to get a restraining order while their abuser was in jail and let the attorneys do their jobs. It wasn't the victims fault he was in jail; it was his actions that put him there.

I recruited volunteers And trained them and gave them support as they began to help out in the court rooms. But for the first five or six months, it was just me doing the work and writing down the necessary steps for getting the case moving—from contacting the woman to literally holding her hand through the entire legal process.

The LA City Attorney's office has multiple offices. In the downtown main office, I had a partitioned off space in which to work. The rest of the offices gave me a space to use when I was there, rarely the same space from week to week. I spent one day a week in each area, building a working relationship with the attorneys as well as the victims, and spending time in court. Once a system was in place, I could recruit volunteers in each area that I could train and supervise while still being available to the attorneys and victims. It was my responsibility to create handouts and see that they were distributed to victims and volunteers. It was most helpful to have volunteers in each of the offices and create a network they could work within.

Occasionally, my recommendations in court were not agreed upon by the assigned attorney, which ruffled a few feathers. But I did what I thought best for the victim.

cacy program was there to assist as many women as we could reach in the system.

Even after I was technically no longer working in the movement, I continued to do interviews on request. I was called on to talk about the O. J. Simpson case before it went to trial. In my opinion, he was guilty. It was a crime of passion, and if it wasn't him, then it was someone very close to him that he was protecting. Since I highly doubt he had the strength of character to go to prison for someone else, I still believe him to be guilty.

> *"Children raised in chaos become adults who live in chaos. Give your child a childhood they don't have to heal from."*
>
> *-Pinterest – Developing Talks*

Chapter Twelve

A Child of Chaos

This is a hard chapter for me to write. My son, Ward, was such a happy baby, bright and beautiful. He was also really big. He came home in clothes a size larger than a typical newborn. He was speaking in sentences at one year. By eighteen months, everything changed. His father became very abusive to me.

In the beginning it was mostly verbal and/or emotional abuse with a little physical hitting thrown in for emphasis. Ward would put his hands over his ears and tell his dad to stop to no avail. Eventually, Michael put a lock on the outside of Ward's bedroom door and would lock him in when

Ward would cling to me to try and intervene. I was told to put him in his room, or it would be worse. Michael would close the door and tell Ward to stay, as if he was a dog. If Ward opened the door, Michael would lock it.

When the abuse wasn't happening, Ward and I would sit in his room and play, or I would read books to him. He had a *Winnie the Pooh* musical lamp, and sometimes I would play it as we marched around the rug singing the song. I sang to him a lot and joined a Mommy and Me class to give him an introduction to learning in a group. It also gave him a chance to make friends.

We walked around the block to get him out of the house, sometimes for an hour or more. Once he got a big wheel, that's what he wanted to do—ride it around and around the block. He was a child who loved freedom. He started climbing over the bars of the crib when he was only eighteen months old. I took out the springs and placed the mattress on the floor to keep him in bed until I got him up, but in another month's time he kicked out the foot of his crib so he could get up whenever he wanted.

He was a big boy for his age, and everyone assumed he was at least two years older than he actually was. His size presented its own set of challenges for him all through school. He was always the biggest and used his size to intimidate and bully the other children if he was afraid they might hurt him. He learned that he didn't actually have to do anything and that the threat itself was enough to keep them away.

fee was reduced. That was a fun experience for us both. We made friends with some of the other moms and children in the class and had play dates at their homes.

After several weeks of bi-weekly classes, each mom was asked to try leaving their child for a short time so they would get used to the process of being away from their mother. When it was my turn, I told Ward that mommy was going to go for a little while. He threw his arms around my neck and sobbed for me to stay. The teacher came and pried him loose, telling him I would be back, but he was terrified and screaming. It took several days of working up to it. He was still screaming and being restrained from running after me, but I finally drove away.

It was hard for me because I knew why he was having such a hard time, and I hadn't shared it with anyone in the group. The teacher convinced me it was in his best interest, so I did it. She said that as soon as I was out of sight, he settled right down and joined in the class activities. That gave me a feeling that she had been right and that he was okay. Months later, she helped me disappear with Ward. The day we left to go into a shelter, the teacher covered for me when Michael came looking for us.

We got a dog—a Great Dane that Ward named Rufus. Michael picked out the dog for his own nefarious purposes, but during the day Rufus was Ward's constant companion. I was concerned at first that a dog that big would break things just walking through the house, but he was incredibly careful. He was fawn colored, a gentle giant, and the size of a small pony. Ward tried to ride him. Unfortunately,

• Beyond Surviving

105

head open on a sprinkler head. He came stumbling in and crawled into bed next to me. When I put my arm around him, I felt something wet and, upon opening my eyes, saw the blood.

I was awake in a second and quickly examined him to find the gash that was still bleeding. Picking him up and throwing some clothes on, I rushed him to his doctor. The pediatrician told me that it would need some stitches, and Ward began thrashing around and screaming hysterically. I couldn't calm him down. The doctor insisted on strapping him onto a cradleboard to keep him still and made me wait outside while he was working on my son. Ward was terrified, and from that moment on, it made future doctor visits close to impossible. It furthered his fear of being restrained or confined, which continued into adulthood.

When he started preschool in Pasadena. there was another boy who, like Ward, was big for his age. I got a call one day that this boy bit Ward, and I had to take him to his pediatrician because the skin was broken, and he was bleeding. She cleaned it up and bandaged his arm. When it came to getting a shot, he went ballistic. She ended up having to call in a nurse who pulled him out from under the exam table where he was cowering like a trapped animal. I was torn between feeling sorry for him and being embarrassed because I couldn't control his behavior.

Once we returned to our house after I was released from the hospital, Ward quickly reconnected with his old friends. He told them I had killed his dad. Perhaps in his six-year-old mind, I killed Michael by leaving the house instead explain in front of Ward and their parents what really happened. It was just a glimpse of what was to come.

I enrolled Ward in a private preschool/kindergarten in our neighborhood. It was close, and they had afterschool daycare so I could work and know Ward was looked after. One day, shortly after Ward started school, the principal called me in and informed me that Ward was a class disruption and not doing well. I explained what had happened in his young life, and they agreed to keep him, but he was failing miserably. He was acting out his anger and confusion and intimidating other students.

When he was ready for first grade, they put him in a regular classroom, but he was, again, too disruptive. They suggested special education and set up a meeting to see if that might be helpful for him. While I was in the waiting room with other moms who were having similar problems, I decided to conduct an impromptu poll. I told the others about what Ward had seen and the domestic violence. It was no surprise that every one of the other moms confirmed that their child had been exposed to violence at home as well.

It was determined that placement in a special education class would be appropriate for Ward. He begged me to keep him in the regular classroom. In his mind, special education was for dummies, and we both knew he wasn't unintelligent. I tried to reason with him, but he hadn't really hit the age of reason, even though he could logically ask questions and pose arguments. In the end, I told him that I wanted him to try it, and if his grades and behavior improved, he

I took him to several child therapists, but he was totally uncooperative with them and even manipulated one of them by staying on the floor playing and not answering any of the doctor's questions. In addition to his behavior, Ward had started sneaking food into his room and was really putting on extra weight. One truth came out at one of his sessions. He was overeating because he "was trying to fill the empty hole inside him." I felt so badly for him but was at my wit's end trying to find a way to help him.

By the time Lynn and I got together, all he would say was "She isn't my dad." He tried a variety of ways to break us apart, but we maintained a united front when dealing with him. Her twenty-four-year-old, mentally disabled daughter, Jamie, moved in with us, and there were times that we were at odds with each other over protecting our own damaged child. Ward used to tease Jamie mercilessly. When I got home from work, Jamie would come flying out of the house to me before I even got out of the car. Screaming "Do you know what your son did?" I, of course, had no idea, so she launched into a frustrated tirade of how he had mistreated her.

Jamie is a sweet, loving young woman, and Ward hurt her feelings time and time again. He would tease her in front of his friends. As in any family, he could abuse her, but if anyone else did, he was her defender. He even called her his sister, but he was not very nice to her. I felt that in his own way, Ward was as disabled as Jamie—but his disability was emotional, and Jamie's was mental. She wasn't capable of defending herself against his verbal assaults. It did it.

When Ward was eleven or twelve, he started running away. This terrified me. I thought he was an innocent that would easily be taken advantage of by older people. But he would spend a little time in juvenile detention facilities or programs, then come home only to run away again.

In desperation, I sent him to live with my brother in Barstow. One of his therapists suggested he needed a male influence in his life and my brother, Chris, agreed to help. Ward wasn't happy there, and I thought it was because Chris wouldn't put up with his nonsense and took appropriate action to stop it. Ward begged me to bring him home, but I just couldn't do it. I was grasping at straws—and I guess he was too in his own way.

My other brother, Steve, took him in for a time. Steve had recently remarried, and his wife, Karen, had three children of her own, so he would have playmates. That didn't work out either. Ward told me if any of the kids said a bad word, Karen would put a hot pepper in their mouths. I have recently had contact with two of her children as adults. They told me that their mom was not nice to any of them. Ward did stay in touch with two of them into his adulthood.

His teen years were a nightmare for both of us. He ran away, got caught, and spent time in juvenile detention or live-in programs for troubled youth. He stole cash, credit cards, and things he could pawn. He even stole Lynn's truck. His lack of control escalated beyond me or anyone trying to help him. He was given chance after chance by the responsible for his actions. I followed his advice, and Ward became an emancipated minor.

When he stole Lynn's truck at the advanced age of 15, he had a friend with him. They went for an extended joy-ride that lasted until he got the truck stuck off-roading in the mountains. Next, they hitchhiked to my brother Steve's, then on to Needles, heading for my parents'. Unfortunately, the boys tried to swim the Colorado River, fully clothed, instead of walking across the bridge, and I got a call from the police. His friend didn't make it. Ward said he tried to help him, but the other kid panicked and kept pushing Ward under the swift current. Ward told the kid to kick off his shoes, that they were weighing him down, but his advice fell on deaf ears. To his credit, Ward stayed where his friend disappeared and called the police.

I was hysterical when I got the call, and Ward was once again locked up for over a year and had to carry the desperate cries of his friend along with all his other emotional, traumatic baggage.

After being released and 18, he ran away to Las Vegas, and came back married to a woman with two kids after being out of touch for over a year. The police came to our door early one morning, pounding on it and threatening to break it down if we didn't get the dogs under control and open the door. They were looking for my son. At that point, Ward and his wife and kids were living in our motorhome in the driveway. After they searched the house, I directed them to the motorhome. They arrested Ward for a parole violation, leaving his wife and children to fend for another tear in detention.

He married again, this time to the mother of my grand-children. She was a waitress at a restaurant he frequented. After they were married he'd work for a time then quit because they weren't paying him enough. Then he started drinking and "borrowing" money. He'd sober up and get a new job, then the cycle would start all over, escalating each time. He became verbally abusive to his wife and children. I started getting frantic phone calls from his wife; he had taken the kids and was out driving around drunk with the kids in the truck, or he was out of control, and could I come talk to him? Eventually, he robbed a bank and ended up in San Quentin for three years. His wife divorced him while he was locked up. He came out with ugly prison tattoos and the nickname of Ogre.

When he came home, he seemed to be changed—more sober and reflective. But it didn't last long, and as soon as he realized his ex-wife, daughter and son weren't going to welcome him back with open arms, he reverted to his old ways and moved in with a friend who joined him in drinking and doing drugs. Then he married again.

He continued cycling through his life until he finally, at twenty-four, became a certified welder. He told me he loved working with fire. He became overeager and thought nothing could harm him. At work, he tried to pick up a solid steel container and tore up his back. He was now getting the good drugs and money from the government in the form of workers compensation. He had back surgery, and, according to him, the doctor botched it. Now he figured changed lawyers a couple of times. Finally, he decided to settle just to get it over with. He got a good faith check for $5,000, went to bed happy, and accidentally overdosed on his pain killers and died on September 30, 2011, only 35 short years old.

We had our first and only real conversation the day before…then he was gone. At that point I was under treatment for Hepatitis C and in a bit of a haze from the drugs I was taking. Lynn woke me up from a nap to tell me he died. For a long time, I think a part of me died too. I also think he had completed his primary task in this life, whatever it was, and was spared further pain.

The things I choose to remember about him were happy moments. His favorite song was "What a Wonderful World," so I like to think somewhere, deep down inside him, the sweet little boy was still there.

"Everything in your life is a reflection of a choice you have made. If you want a different result, make a different choice."

-Quotespedia.org Author unknown

Chapter Thirteen

It's Your Choice!

Choose to learn from wise teachers, listen to their words and incorporate what you learn into your life, to live in the present and appreciate the little things that glue everything else together. Invest your time learning what inspires you and what makes you happy. I've always been interested in looking into different spiritual practices and alternative healing methods. It was not really a surprise to me that all the spiritual paths I've explored generally share the same basic lessons with love being at the center of everything.

Write down your feelings. Journal, diary, list, whatever feels best to you. There are many books out in the world now we'll ever do." A favorite quote of mine by Brené Brown.

Don't mistake jealousy as a signal that he cares and feel flattered. It's really a signal that he is insecure and afraid of losing you. That can make him dangerous.

Along the way you will meet new people that appreciate you for who you are. You will have a different perspective on life and will find people who are willing, not only to help you along the way, but who are happy to be there for you when the lingering doubts creep into your mind.

Don't be afraid to open your heart to love again. The willingness to open my heart brought me my partner of 39 years. I do believe that those of us who have been hurt are loving people, but too many of us are afraid to open up again. Don't let that be you! Love is the greatest gift we have to share with one another. Pay attention to who you let in. You will find you have learned the power of discernment; you will know when someone is lying; you will have the power to choose to walk away from the liar; you can confront the lie and find the truth. It's your choice that determines the outcome.

"The U.S. Surgeon General has declared that attacks by male partners are the number one cause of injury to women between the ages of fifteen and forty-four. The American Medical Association reports that one woman out of three will be a victim of violence by her husband or boyfriend at some point in her life" reported in the book *Why Does He Do That: Inside the Minds of Angry and Controlling Men* by Lundy Bancroft.

insecure and afraid of losing you. That can make him dangerous. And remember that every time you forgive an abuser when they apologize for hurting you, you are giving them permission to continue abusing you.

Something most others won't tell you is that when you move out, it can be even more dangerous for you. This is when the most severe violence can occur because he can't see your every move and feels his control slipping. You hear about it on the news almost every night. Do it anyway—you need to take that chance! Staying not only affects you, it affects your child or children horribly.

You can get a restraining order, which is a one form of legal protection, but be aware that it is only a piece of paper. If your abuser has no respect for the law, it's not going to protect you. If you get a restraining order then willingly let your abuser back into your life, you have voided the order and no help will be forth coming.

It was no surprise for me to learn that almost all women who are in prison for violent crimes are there for either defending themselves from an abusive man or were used by their abuser to commit the crime. The law still doesn't take the abuse suffered by a woman into consideration if they make a preemptive strike instead of waiting until they are attacked again to fight back. Prosecutors insist that the woman was in no immediate danger, but it may have been the only time she felt safe enough to handle the situation when she realized that if she didn't attack first, he was going to kill her.

interest. You can call it whatever works for you—intuition, guidance, just knowing—it all boils down to the same thing. Your subconscious always protects you based on what you believe to be true. Your gut already knows the truth.

It's interesting to me that so many men try to silence us by attacking the throat, which just happens to be the chakra of our will. Slashing, choking, and strangling seem to be an unconscious attempt to silence us, to keep us from speaking our truth. Sharing our truth gives others hope. It's why this book was written. If I can change, so can you.

I'm happy to tell you that men waking up to the realization that they are the problem and are actually getting involved with changing violent patterns. There are books and organizations that encourage men to recognize domestic violence as a man's problem. They meet, write, or blog to discuss how it's been seen as a woman's problem, but if men stopped themselves and learned new ways to deal with their anger and disappointment, there would be less violence in the home. It's been a long time coming, but it's here now and will continue to grow in society's consciousness.

Choose to learn from wise teachers—listen to their words and incorporate what you learn into your life—to live in the present and appreciate the little things that glue everything else together. Invest your time learning what inspires you and what makes you happy. I've always been interested in looking into different spiritual practices and alternative healing methods. It was not really a surprise to me that all the spiritual paths I've explored generally share the same basic lessons, with love being at the center of everything.

now that encourage this way of healing. "Owning our stories and loving ourselves through that process is the bravest thing we'll ever do." A favorite quote of mine by Brené Brown. One good way to start is to write about something you smell, you hear, you see, you touch, or you taste. Use your imagination. If nothing awakens your senses, think about how a flower smells, a bird sings, a cloud drifts by, a smooth stone feels, or biting into a ripe piece of fruit tastes.

Along the way, you will meet new people that appreciate you for who you are. You will have a different perspective on life and will find people who are willing not only to help you along the way but who are happy to be there for you when the lingering doubts creep into your mind.

Pay attention to who you let in. You will find you have learned the power of discernment; you will know when someone is lying. You will have the power to choose to walk away from the liar or you can confront the lie and find the truth. It's your choice that determines the outcome.

Don't be afraid to open your heart to love again. The willingness to open my heart brought me my partner of thirty-nine years. I do believe that those of us who have been hurt are loving people, but too many of us are afraid to open up again. Don't let that be you! Love is the greatest gift we have to share with one another.

Dream again and dare to follow your dreams. Dreams lead to great adventures and wonderful discoveries. Years later, you will look back and wonder why it took so long for you to arrive at your truth again. When you're in the

Dyer, said to forget the trauma, but keep the lesson. It's good advice.

You are resilient. You are stronger than you think. Look at what you've survived already. Believe in yourself again. You are not just what has hurt you, so be as powerful as you truly are.

Carolyn Myss said, "Choice is a fundamental power of the human experience." If you don't like where you are, you have the power of choosing something different.

Along the way, I've been inspired by so many bits of wisdom that appeared when they were needed most. If you pay attention to what's going on around you, you will experience similar synchronicities. Just keep your eyes open and be amazed!

You don't have to do this alone. There are many support groups available to help you move forward. For starters, there is the National Coalition Against Domestic Violence. They can refer you to a local coalition if you prefer something closer to home. You have rights and NCADV can enumerate them for you. If all else fails, Google it!

My parting words are simply this: It's your life, go out and live it! Everyday take another step and don't forget to turn around and offer your hand to the person behind you. Thank you for taking this journey with me. I hope you find your own journey as amazing and satisfying as you can imagine it to be. What will you choose for your life?

Things to Remember

- Look at your reasons for staying. It wasn't until after many years of study that I realized I always had a choice to leave the abuse behind. Staying as long as I did was also a choice—I just wasn't aware I was making one.

- Staying for the children is a bad choice. They will grow up thinking this is how a normal family lives their life. They resent how their dad treats their mom and grow up either becoming abusive themselves (because they think it's the normal way to be), or thinking it will never happen to them because they won't allow themselves to get involved with anyone. They may be being abused themselves—especially if they're girls.

- Staying because you don't think you can make it on your own is also a bad choice. There are plenty of people and agencies that will help you get on your feet, and you're stronger than you think. Look at what you've survived so far.

Beyond Surviving

is another bad choice. Children would rather be in a safe, loving home. Yes, they'll whine about how dad always got them stuff, but it's only stuff. It can't love them, it can't make them happy, and it can't make them feel safe.

- Verbal abuse can be as painful (and sometimes more so) than physical abuse. I learned this firsthand. My late husband had a degree in psychology and used it against me. There's an article by Audre Lord I used as a handout titled "The Bruise That Doesn't Heal" that covers this one very well.

- Make a plan. Whether you do this on your own or have family or friends that will help, if you have a plan in place, it will give you direction for the next step in your life.

- Get out! Go somewhere he won't find you, and give yourself the time and support to start making plans for a better future for yourself and your children, if you have them.

- Leave the problem behind but keep the lesson learned. Reflect on the issue and look for the lesson. Once you find it, you'll never have to repeat it because if you find yourself in a situation that feels uncomfortably familiar, you'll know what to do.

worth it. I strongly recommend Louise Hay's book *You Can Heal Yourself*. It's beautiful and soothing and takes you step by step.

- You have to put the past behind you and move on. You can't change it, so why waste time dwelling on it.

- Forgive him for his behavior—he didn't know any better. There's a very good chance that he grew up around abuse and thought that his behavior was appropriate for a husband and father. I'm not suggesting you have to stay with him but if you don't forgive him it will continue to hurt you.

- Forgive yourself for staying—it was just a bad choice.

- Educate yourself in every way you can: finish school if you haven't already; learn something new every day; learn a skill; hone your talent; read inspiring books or magazine articles; recognize that you're on a journey.

- Keep putting one foot in front of the other so you keep moving forward.

- If you stumble or fall, get up and keep moving. It's better than what you left behind. You'll find that soon it becomes a habit.

that even if you fake a great big grin, your brain releases endorphins and you feel better.

- Happiness is a choice and so is unhappiness. It's that simple. Stop looking for something outside of you to make you happy. It's an inside job.

- Live in the present. The past will drag you down and the future will take care of itself. I'm sure you've heard the saying that the past is over and can't be changed and the future isn't here yet, so stay in the present which is a new gift every day.

- If things happen that you don't like in your life, the only thing you can change is your reaction to them. If a choice you made no longer feels good to you, remember that you can always try something different.

- Love is the most important thing you will ever learn and is all that really matters. Everything else is replaceable.

Resources

POV - Peace Over Violence 24/7 LA Rape & Battering Hotline 626.793.3385 | 310.392.8381 | 213.626.3393 Serves, Women, Children, Teens, Men and Disabled.

Sean Smith Coaching men as well as women (805) 552-4423

National Hotline For Domestic Violence (800) 799-7233

NCADV – National Coalition Against Domestic Violence (303) 839-1852

NOMORE.org – Organization to support No More Domestic Violence

NRCDV – National Resource Center on Domestic Violence (800) 537-2238

Futures Without Violence (415) 678-5500, (202) 595-7382

Susan Ball, REAL Recovery After Abuse

susan@susanball.ca

www.recoveryafterabuse.ca

NNEDV: National Network To End Domestic Violence, Washington, DC (202) 543-5566

Womenslaw.org

Techsafety.org

GAFTR Global Association for Trauma Recovery (678) 568-9191

Tracey Osborne CEO/Founder tracey@gaftr.org

http://gaftr.org

VAWnet The Online Resource Center on Violence against Women (800) 537-2238

There is a growing awareness that men, in partnership with women, can play a significant role in ending violence against women. This has led to an increase in programs and activities that focus on men's roles in preventing violence against women. Men's anti-violence programs are informed by the understanding that violence against women hurts women and that men can have an important influence on reducing violence by changing their own attitudes and behavior and by intervening to prevent other men's violence.

MADVAC – Men Against Domestic Violence Action Coalition

Check your local area for contact number

MSV – Men Stopping Violence (404) 270-9894

Acknowledgements

This has been a work of love for anyone who has been through an abusive relationship and come through it stronger than they could ever imagine, who have written their pain and reached a hand back to help the next one in line by sharing their stories by the thousands.

I would like to thank my publisher, Lisa M. Umina at Halo Publishing, Int'l, for supporting me through the maze that is book publishing and to Jenn T Grace for introducing us. I'm also extremely grateful for the editing polish of Lauren Bittrich, Kaye Falls, and Sherrie Clark all made my story flow.

I also need to acknowledge Marjon Vahdatiasl, Peggie Reyna, Sherry Byrne, Janice June Guerrero, Judy Wells-McConnell, Ed Zeiser, Maggie Lynch, Rhett Nichols, and Jean-Paul Goodrich along with hundreds of other women and men who encouraged and cheered me on while I wrote my story.

I could not have written and re-lived this experience without the support and love of my family and friends. They gave me the time and space I needed along with their throughout our life together, but for holding my hand and reading my first draft of everything.